Islam

Understanding the History, Beliefs, and Culture

ISSUES IN FOCUS TODAY

Julie Williams

Enslow Publishers, Inc.
40 Industrial Road
Box 398
Berkeley Heights, NJ 07922
USA
http://www.enslow.com

Acknowledgments

The author is grateful to Ismail Kashkoush of the Islamic Center of the Lehigh Valley, who very generously provided information and materials on the Muslim faith, the history of Islam, and what it is like to be a Muslim in the United States. Thanks also to Tamim Ansary and Munir Shaikh, who read and commented upon earlier versions of the mansucript.

Quotations from the Qur'an in translation are from Muhammad Ali, The Holy Qur'an, Arabic Text with English Translation and Commentary *(Dublin, Ohio: Ahmadiyya Anjuman Isha'at Islam Lahore Inc., USA, 2002); used with permission.*

Library of Congress Cataloging-in-Publication Data

Williams, Julie.
 Islam: understanding the history, beliefs, and culture / Julie Williams.
   p. cm.—(Issues in focus today)
 Summary: "Discusses the religion of Islam, including its origins, belief system and prac-tices, and the culture it has created in many countries throughout the world"—Provided by publisher.
 Includes bibliographical references and index.
 ISBN-13: 978-0-7660-2686-5
 ISBN-10: 0-7660-2686-8
 1. Islam—Juvenile literature. 2. Islam—Doctrines—Juvenile literature. 3. Islam—Essence, genius, nature—Juvenile literature. I. Title.
  BP161.3.W56 3008
  297—dc22

                              2007028483

Printed in the United States of America

10 9 8 7 6 5 4 3 2 1

To Our Readers: We have done our best to make sure all Internet addresses in this book were active and appropriate when we went to press. However, the author and the publisher have no control over and assume no liability for the material available on those Internet sites or on other Web sites they may link to. Any comments or suggestions can be sent by e-mail to comments@enslow.com or to the address on the back cover.

Illustration Credits: AP/Wide World, pp. 1, 3, 31, 38, 42, 50, 56, 60, 63, 70, 82, 93, 97, 99, 103; Brynn Brujin/*Saudi Aramco* World/PADIA, pp. 3, 46; Corel Corp., p. 74; Library of Congress, pp. 35, 68; Shutterstock, pp. 3, 5, 15, 19, 27, 95.

Cover Illustration: Shutterstock (large photo); BananaStock (small inset photo).

Contents

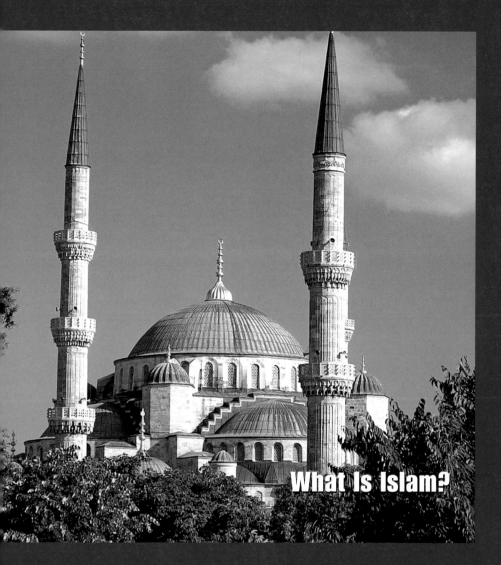

What Is Islam?

Islam is one of the great religions of the world. Today it is the fastest growing religion in the world and has over one billion followers. Only Christianity is larger. Muslims live in every country in the world. Most countries in the Middle East are predominantly Muslim, but Muslims make up the majority population in at least fifty-six countries.[1]

Over one-third of the population of Africa follows Islam.[2] Muslims constitute significant minorities in many Western countries. There are 1.3 million Muslims in Great Britain, 3.2 million in Germany, and 4.2 million in France, according to a recent estimate.[3] As many as 7 million Muslims live in the

United States.[4] You may be surprised to learn that China has a substantial Muslim population, as many as 120 million.[5]

The name "Islam" means "submission to God." Muslims believe that only God is worthy of worship, and that no other beings deserve to be worshipped. They believe that the chief prophet of Islam, Muhammad, was the last prophet God sent to the world. They view him as a great man, but since he was a human being, they do not worship him. This is the reason Muslims do not approve of the term "Mohammedan," which has been used by some Westerners to describe followers of Islam. One who follows Islam is properly known as a "Muslim," meaning "one who submits to God."

Although Islam, like other monotheistic faiths, arose in the Middle East, today Muslims come from all racial and ethnic backgrounds. Many Muslims follow Islam because they were born into the faith, but Islam has always welcomed converts as well. Many people in Eastern and Western countries embrace Islam. It has played a significant role in world affairs for many centuries, and it currently constitutes an important religious, cultural, and political factor in every country around the globe.

Islamic Civilization

Islamic history is considered to have begun in 622 C.E. This is the year Muhammad moved from the city of Mecca to the nearby city of Medina. He was invited by the city's residents to become their political and spiritual leader. After Muhammad's

Dating Definitions

C.E. means "common era"; B.C.E. means "before the common era." These terms correspond to the B.C. and A.D. in the dating system that is based on the birth and death of Jesus. However, they are often used without a specific religious connotation. Muslims and Jews use their own system of dates in their religious calendars.

death, Islam spread quickly over the Middle East, Asia, southern Europe, and northern Africa. Muslim leaders ruled large parts of Spain, Turkey, Iran, Iraq, northern Africa, and northern India at various times from 632 to 1922. Five powerful Muslim empires made their marks on the world during this time: the Abbasid dynasty, centered in Iran, which existed from 750 to 1258; the Muslim Spanish empire, which ruled parts of the Iberian peninsula from 750 to 1492; the Moghul empire, which oversaw much of the lands of India and Pakistan from 1526 to 1857; the Safavids, who ruled the area now called Iran from 1501 to 1722; and the Ottoman empire, centered in Turkey, whose sultans reigned over a vast area stretching across North Africa, eastern Europe, and much of the Middle East from 1300 to 1922.

Most countries in the Middle East are predominantly Muslim, and Muslims make up the majority population in at least fifty-six countries.

Muslim culture, including scientific achievements, legal scholarship, literature, art, and architecture, rose to great heights in the centuries following Muhammad's death. We owe the discovery of algebra to a Muslim mathematician, Muhammad ibn Musa al-Khwarzimi (790–850). In addition to their own significant contributions, Muslim scholars kept Greek, Persian, and Babylonian philosophy; mathematics; science and other studies alive in the East during the Western Dark Ages.

Islamic art excelled in the areas of calligraphy, which is an artistic style of writing in the Arabic script, and geometric designs based on mathematics. Examples of Muslim architecture, such as the Taj Mahal in India, are admired throughout the world. Muslim writers have produced famous works such as *A Thousand and One Nights* and *The Rubaiyat of Omar Khayyam*. One of Shakespeare's greatest characters, Othello, is a Muslim.

In the past, Muslim governments created conditions in many areas across the world that allowed for the growth of culture. Muslims are understandably proud of this and remember the great accomplishments of Islamic civilization with admiration and, sometimes, sadness that those times have passed.

Muslim Religion and Muslim Culture: Are They the Same?

Religious practices and social customs overlap in every community. Non-Muslims sometimes become confused about whether a Muslim is doing something because it is a religious duty or because it is part of his or her culture. For example, most Muslims observe the religious duties of praying five times a day while facing the direction of Mecca, attending group prayer at an Islamic center just after noon on Fridays, and fasting during daylight hours in the month of Ramadan. However, varied customs in areas such as styles of clothing, methods of finding a marriage partner, and women's roles in public are found in Muslim communities around the world. They originate in a person's family or national background or from personal choice. They are not dictated by religion, although religion may influence them. They are culturally determined.

Even in countries that are predominantly Muslim, religious and cultural habits combine in different ways. In Saudi Arabia, for example, religious leaders have decreed that women must wear scarves that cover their hair and neck. Yet in Turkey, whose population is 98 percent Muslim, the headscarf is banned in universities and government jobs.

Sometimes religion and culture clash, especially in countries where Muslims are in the minority. Some employers may not want to give their Muslim employees time away from work to attend Friday prayers because their absence will disrupt business activities. Friends may not understand when a Muslim fasting during Ramadan gets tired more easily at the end of the day.

Since the beginning of Islam, Muslims and non-Muslims have been able to live cooperatively side-by-side in most cases.

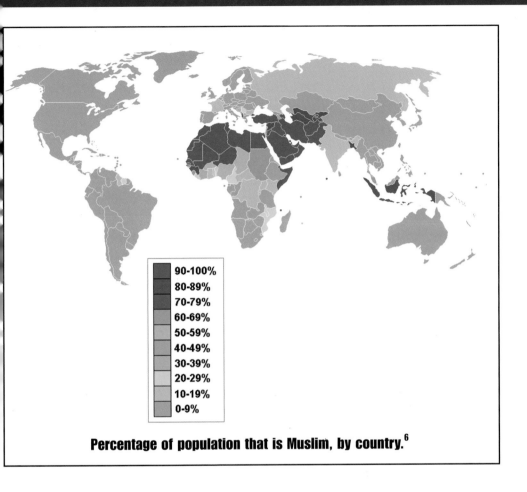

| 90-100% |
| 80-89% |
| 70-79% |
| 60-69% |
| 50-59% |
| 40-49% |
| 30-39% |
| 20-29% |
| 10-19% |
| 0-9% |

Percentage of population that is Muslim, by country.[6]

When Muslim leaders conquered territories outside Arabia in the late seventh and early eighth centuries, Jews, Christians, and others were not forced to convert to Islam. Muslim rulers allowed them to continue practicing their religion. These groups paid a special tax to the Muslim authorities, who in exchange took the responsibility to protect these communities as they would Muslims from attack by hostile forces.[7]

Today, Muslims and non-Muslims generally respect each other. However, when they do not know much about one another's customs and beliefs, their ignorance can breed fear, which may grow into hostility and violence. Especially in countries where Islam is a minority religion, Muslims may be considered strange or even dangerous.

Terrorism and Islam: Is There a Connection?

Relationships between Muslims and non-Muslims were rocked by the attacks of September 11, 2001, when nineteen men claiming to act in the name of Islam hijacked three airplanes and flew them into the World Trade Center and the Pentagon, buildings that symbolized American economic, military, and political power. A fourth plane, believed to have been headed for the capitol building in Washington, D.C., crashed in Pennsylvania when the passengers took it back from the hijackers. The nineteen men were part of a small number of Muslims who feel that political and cultural forces in the non-Muslim world threaten Muslims. They have decided to use terrorism as

Women at the Tomb of Hussein in Iran. Muslim art of this period, as shown in the intricate mosaic on the walls, was based on geometric designs.

a way to spread their message. Terrorism has been defined in many different ways, but it normally includes the unlawful use of violence (or the threat of violence) against people who are not military combatants, intended to create fear, for political, social, or religious ends. These Muslim terrorists claim a religious justification for their actions, saying that the Qur'an requires a jihad, or holy war, against anyone who poses a threat to Muslims and Islam.

Most Muslims believe that terrorism is not the right way to effect change in the world. The Qur'an allows Muslims to fight for just causes such as self-defense, but emphasizes mercy and tolerance. Muslim scholars point out that the verses in the Qur'an cited by the terrorists as justification for their actions were only intended to be advice for specific battles that Muhammad was involved in. Shirin Ebadi, the first Muslim woman to receive the Nobel Peace Prize, has said, "You can be sure that if someone is killed in the name of Islam, the name of Islam was misused."[8] However, even some moderate Muslims find themselves wondering if at least some violent activities are justified in bringing attention to what they perceive as unjust treatment of Muslims.[9]

Consequences of Terrorism

The United States and its allies, including several Muslim countries, have tried to prevent future terrorist attacks by launching a "War on Terror." The U.S. government detains those it suspects of being terrorists. Sometimes this has meant holding people in jail simply because they are Muslim or were born in the Middle East. Suspects have been held without bail for several years. In the months following September 11, the President authorized monitoring of potentially suspicious telephone calls without court orders. The United States invaded Iraq in 2003 because the President believed that the Iraqi president, Saddam Hussein, was encouraging terrorism and building weapons of mass destruction. The American public is split on whether it feels these actions are justified in the face of terrorist threats or if they constitute an unreasonable invasion of privacy and excessive force.[10] Many members of the public are confused about the purpose of new security legislation enacted after September 11, such as the Patriot Act.[11]

Some Muslims feel they are all being lumped together into a group called "religious extremists." After September 11, the United States instituted new laws forcing Muslims from foreign countries to register with the Immigration and Naturalization Service and be fingerprinted. Airport security gives Middle Eastern travelers especially thorough searches. Since September 11, highly qualified Muslim foreigners who have skills to bring to the American workplace have been denied visas. Muslim students also have more difficulty obtaining permission to study in the United States than they did before September 11.[12]

Ignorance has a profound effect on Americans' ideas about Muslims and violence. A July 2005 survey of Americans found that people who had never met a Muslim had more negative

Al Jazeera Television

The Al Jazeera satellite television network has become well known, even infamous, all around the world for showing videos of blindfolded prisoners begging for their lives surrounded by masked gunmen. But Al Jazeera is much more than controversial videos. Al Jazeera started in the country of Qatar in 1996. The name means "the island/the peninsula." It is the main television station to receive statements from radical Islamic leaders such as Osama bin Laden. This causes some Americans to view the station with distrust. However, many residents of Middle Eastern countries trust Al Jazeera more than the television news from their own government-controlled stations. In 2006, only ten years after it began, Al Jazeera drew an estimated 50 million viewers worldwide. It has received awards for its courage in broadcasting open discussions of political controversies in spite of death threats.[13]

views of Muslims in general than did those who knew Muslims personally. Muslims in the United States report feeling less comfortable after September 11 than they did before among people who do not know them personally. The survey also found that a large number of Americans believe that Islam is a religion that encourages violence.[14] Hate crimes against Muslims in the United States rose more than 50 percent between 2003 and 2004.[15]

Some Americans are so uninformed and frightened of "Islamic" terrorism that they lash out at anyone who might be Middle Eastern or Asian. Four days after the September 11 attacks, the Sikh owner of a gas station was shot and killed in Mesa, Arizona. The gunman then drove to another gas station and shot at the owner, a Lebanese American. Finally he went to a home he used to own and fired at the occupants, a family from Afghanistan. The shooter, later identified as Frank Roque, told people after September 11 that he was going to "kill some towelheads." He was convicted of murder and sentenced to death in 2003.[16]

The Need for Understanding

In a 2003 poll, almost two thirds of Americans admitted that they knew little about the Islamic religion.[17] This lack of understanding can have dangerous consequences. Immediately after the bombing of an Oklahoma City federal building in April 1995, news sources reported sightings of Muslim men at the scene. A former member of Congress announced that the bombing was undoubtedly the work of Middle Eastern terrorists.[18] Two American men who had no Middle Eastern or Muslim backgrounds were later convicted of that crime, but not before shots were fired into an Oklahoma City mosque and Muslim residents were harassed. Similarly, many reports of Islamic terrorism came in when TWA Flight 800 crashed in 1996 off the eastern seaboard. The cause of the crash was eventually found to be mechanical failure.[19] But to some Americans, these incidents still called up the specter of "Islamic terrorists."

The lack of information and the suspicion it breeds go both ways. Some Muslims who move to the United States are upset when they see Americans dressing in a revealing manner, using bad language, and not showing respect to their elders. They understandably resist the idea that American culture is in every way "better" than the one they have left, even if they have come to the United States seeking political freedom and economic opportunity. In their daily lives, they can find their neighbors' curious stares at their headscarves tedious. They may grow tired of explaining to anxious non-Muslims that they go to the mosque on Fridays to pray, not to plan terror attacks. They may withdraw into their own community and have little to do with non-Muslims.

This book provides information on Islam and Muslim beliefs and ways of life for students in the United States in the hope of increasing communication between Muslims and non-Muslims. Only with communication can understanding and tolerance occur.

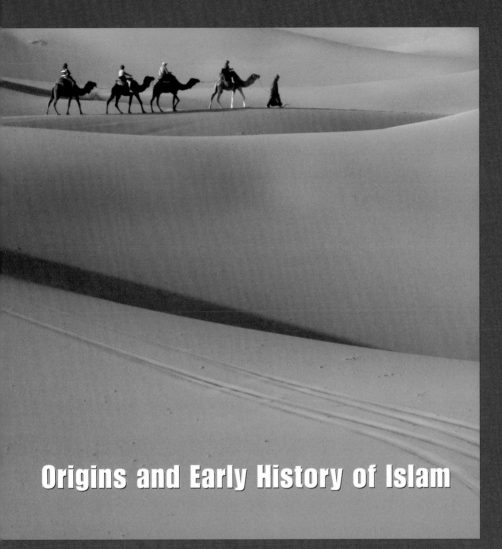

Origins and Early History of Islam

A sad little boy cried in the Arabian desert city of Mecca. Muhammad was six years old and already an orphan. His father, Abdallah, had died before Muhammad was born in 570 C.E. Now his mother, Amina, had passed away. His family had been wealthy and respected in earlier generations but now faced the grim specter of poverty. What would happen to little Muhammad?

The orphan ended up in the home of his uncle, the merchant Abu Talib. He took Muhammad with him on his journeys but was not able to give him a formal education. Muhammad never learned to read or write. As the boy grew up, he got a reputation for intelligence and, above all, honesty. In 595, because of his reputation for trustworthiness, a widowed merchant named Khadija asked Muhammad to take one of her caravans on a trading voyage. He did so successfully, and Khadija was so impressed with him that she asked him to marry her. Muhammad was twenty-five years old, Khadija forty. The marriage was considered unusual by many at the time, but it was happy. The couple had six children, and remained close until Khadija's death in 619.

The world in which the boy Muhammad grew to manhood was harsh and challenging. No organized government existed to provide security to travelers. The nomadic Bedouin tribes constantly fought with each other. The Arabs were suspicious of the few Jewish and Christian groups who inhabited the area. The Arabs of Mecca had learned to live in the forbidding desert by putting their tribal group or clan at the center of their value system. In such a dry, harsh climate, safety could only be found in numbers. The duty of each person was to protect the group. Sometimes this meant killing those who dishonored the tribe. Raids on other tribes were also common as a way to get food and essential goods.

The Meccans worshipped a host of deities connected with the Ka'aba, a box-shaped granite building in the city, forty feet square and fifty feet tall, housing a black, basketball-sized meteorite believed to have been sent down from heaven. People from all parts of the Arabian peninsula made pilgrimages to the Ka'aba. Muhammad always had great respect for the Ka'aba, and worshipped there frequently. The chief of the gods at the Ka'aba was called "Allah," properly spelled "al-Llah," meaning "the god." Christian Arabs as well as Muslims speak of God in Arabic using the word Allah, just as Spanish speakers refer to God as Dios.

Recite! Read!

By the time Muhammad was forty years old, he had started to make regular spiritual retreats. He often went to a cave in a mountain named Hira, spending days in solitude and prayer. One day was different, however. In the year 610 C.E., according to tradition, Muhammad sat in the cave, praying and meditating. Suddenly, the tradition says, he saw an angel and heard a voice commanding him, "Recite! Read!" The illiterate merchant was confused. He told the angel that he could not, but the angel continued to demand that he recite and read. Muhammad refused until the angel held him so tightly he could not breathe. Finally, the first words of what would be called the Qur'an came from his lips: "Recite in the name of your God who created!" (Sura 96:1)

Muhammad ran from the cave in terror. He sought counsel and comfort from his wife. When he had finished describing what he had seen and heard, Khadija knew that Muhammad had experienced something extraordinary. She took him to see her cousin, a devout Christian. This man, Waraqa, confirmed enthusiastically that Muhammad was a prophet for his people.

Muhammad received revelations he ascribed to God, coming through the angel Gabriel, for the rest of his life. The experiences could be physically painful for him; sometimes he would faint. He described feeling strong vibrations as if a bell were ringing, shaking him with its powerful sound. Sometimes he had to struggle to hear and understand the messages. Other times, he said, he could see an angel and hear words clearly.

Numbering in the Qur'an

The Qur'an is divided into 114 chapters, called suras. They are arranged by length, not by subject matter or when Muhammad first recited them. The verses within each sura are numbered.

Muhammad did not at first feel that he was starting a "new religion." He felt that the message he received was a continuation of the teachings of the earlier prophets recognized by Jews and Christians. The Qur'an contains many chapters about the Biblical prophets, including Noah, Abraham, Moses, and David, and about Jesus and his family. Muslims call the Jews, Christians, and themselves "People of the Book," in recognition of their shared heritage.

Muhammad started cautiously. He did not rush out and shout his message from the rooftops. He kept quiet as he struggled to accept that he had been called as a prophet of God. Then he began preaching what he believed the angel had told him, but only to certain members of his tribe, the Quraysh. The message encouraged people to believe that there was only one god and that they should practice responsibility toward family and the whole of society. Soon a small group of followers of Islam, as this religion was called, were praying together twice a day and reciting the verses of the Qur'an.

Muhammad tried to reach the rest of the members of his tribe. Many were unwilling to abandon the beliefs of their ancestors and did not listen. Some of the earliest converts outside Muhammad's family and friends were young people, as well as members of clans with little political or personal power. They were attracted to the message of the Qur'an because of its strong emphasis on justice for all people. This message threatened the traditional tribal structure of Mecca. A number of families were torn apart as some members proclaimed their allegiance to Islam while others did not.[1]

The Qur'an

Muhammad recited the words he received to his close associates. The Arabs had a strong oral tradition, and most poetry was recited aloud from memory rather than being read from a book. Thus, Muhammad's friends had no difficulty in memorizing the verses of revelation that were recited to them. Eventually, those who were literate began writing down the words.

The revelations put together are called the Qur'an, meaning "reading, recitation." Muslims believe that the Qur'an is the unchanged, direct word of God. They believe that it has been unaltered, unlike the Hebrew or Christian scriptures which, they say, have been changed by human intervention over the centuries. The Qur'an is not a historical narration, but a collection of messages that encourage, warn, advise, and call to action. It covers every aspect of life, moving between religious instruction and practical advice, sometimes with bewildering speed. But its central focal point is always God. An official

Muslims believe that the Qur'an is the unchanged, direct word of God. Copies of the Qur'an are therefore treated with the greatest reverence.

compilation of the Qur'an was made around 650 C.E., after Muhammad's death, by one of his successors.[2]

Copies of the Qur'an itself are treated with utmost respect by all Muslims because they are considered to contain the literal word of God. When reports surfaced that United States troops guarding Muslim prisoners at Guantanamo Bay, Cuba, may have placed copies of the Qur'an on toilets and even flushed away one copy, demonstrations and protests broke out all around the world.[3]

The Qur'an is composed in a beautiful, literary form of Arabic. Stories tell that some early Muslims were converted to Islam as they listened to the extraordinary grandeur of the words.[4] Muslims believe that the Qur'an cannot be fully comprehended except in its original language. Because of the importance of the Qur'an in Islam, Muslims use many Arabic words when practicing or talking about their religion, even though most Muslims do not speak Arabic as their native language. Muslim children learn to read the Qur'an and other religious texts in Arabic at religious schools.

Hijra—the Move to Medina

The little group of Muslims continued to grow in secret for about three years. In 613 C.E., Muhammad began preaching more publicly and condemning the worship of deities other than God. His rejection of the pagan traditions aroused great fear among the Arabs. His revolutionary demand struck at the heart of the tribal system because it required the people to pledge allegiance not to the tribe but to God. This meant a change in the most basic structure of Arab society.

Initially, the Meccans boycotted and persecuted the Muslims. They also tried to bribe Muhammad with promises of wealth and political power, but he did not abandon his message. Tensions grew to the point that the Meccans plotted to kill Muhammad. The city of Yathrib lay to the north of Mecca.

Smaller than Mecca, it suffered from constant tribal conflict. Some leaders in Yathrib had met Muhammad on their pilgrimages to Mecca and were impressed with his leadership. They asked him to become the chief of the city, and he agreed. Muhammad and a group of Muslims moved to Yathrib in 622. Yathrib was renamed Medinat un Nabi, "the city of the Prophet," in his honor. The name is usually shortened to "Medina," which means "the city" in Aramaic. Muhammad's move is called the hijra, or "migration." Because of its importance, 622 C.E. is counted as the first year in the Islamic calendar.

Muhammad's beloved wife Khadija had died in 619. A year later, Muhammad took another wife. Over the course of his life, he married a total of thirteen different women. All but one were widowed or divorced, and most already had children. Women at this time were helpless if they did not have a father or husband to protect them. Muhammad's marriages protected these women and their children and also, in some cases, cemented political alliances.

During Muhammad's time in Medina, he continued to receive revelations he believed came through the angel Gabriel. Many of these messages addressed circumstances faced by the Muslim community, such as political alliances, judging people fairly, and when it was proper to fight on behalf of Muslim beliefs. The leaders of Mecca saw the fledgling Muslim community as a political and religious rival that had to be destroyed before it succeeded in overthrowing the entire tribal system. Each side raided the other's caravans, and several key battles took place over several years. Finally, a truce was negotiated, and when the Meccans violated it in 630, Muhammad returned to Mecca and took control of the city without any bloodshed. Those who had opposed Muhammad were given amnesty and spared from retribution, and many Meccans converted to Islam.

In March 632, Muhammad became increasingly ill. He

experienced raging headaches and fainted frequently. He was able to give one powerful address, called the "Farewell Sermon," to about one hundred thousand followers. He died on June 8, 632. In the Islamic calendar, this is the twelfth day of the month Rabi, in the year 10.

Example of the Life of the Prophet

Muhammad's life is considered by Muslims to be the example of a perfect life. Records of his statements are called hadith. These were collected by various people during and after Muhammad's life. Over time, the collected sayings were put together and reviewed.

Imam Bukhari was one of the early collectors of hadith. He traveled all over the Middle East looking for people who might have heard something Muhammad had said, or who knew someone who had known Muhammad. By the time he died in 870 C.E., he had gathered more than six hundred thousand hadith. However, he considered only seventy-three hundred of them to be sufficiently reliable to include in his book of hadith.[5]

The sum total of sayings and actions gathered in the hadith and other sources is called the "Sunnah." The Sunnah is a record of the prophet's way of life, his words, and actions in everyday life and in religious practices. Muslims feel that the Qur'an must be interpreted through the Sunnah. The prophet himself said in his Farewell Sermon to the Muslims that they should hold fast to the Qur'an and the example of his own life so that they would never go astray.

Islam After the Death of Muhammad.

Muhammad died without naming a successor. Many thought that his cousin and son-in-law, Ali, was the logical next leader. However, the elderly Abu Bakr, one of the prophet's earliest and most loyal followers, was chosen by the majority. He led the community for only two years before dying in 634 C.E. Shortly before his death, he held a meeting and the group chose Umar to succeed him.

During the ten years of Umar's leadership, Muslim armies defeated forces of the Byzantine Sasanid empires, and Muslim rule expanded outside Arabia to include Egypt, Syria, parts of Iraq, and Jerusalem. Umar was assassinated after ruling for ten years. The Muslims chose as the new ruler another close companion of the prophet, Uthman, the husband of one of Muhammad's daughters. Uthman had a standardized copy of the complete Qur'an issued to all the provinces. However, corruption grew during his tenure, and he was murdered after twelve years by dissatisfied soldiers.

At this point, Ali was named leader. Ali replaced all of the corrupt leaders who had given Uthman so much trouble. One of them, Mu'awiya, tricked Ali into negotiating the leadership of all Muslims. Some of Ali's followers were so angry at their leader that they sent an assassin who stabbed him to death in 661. Mu'awiya then became the leader. Now, instead of leaders chosen by a group of elders, the Muslim state was led by a king and his successors.[6]

Shi'a and Sunni

The events in the thirty years after the death of Muhammad were responsible for dividing Islam into two major camps that exist to this day. These two groups share basic religious beliefs and practices, but they have markedly different assumptions about how to govern the community of Muslims, the ummah, and who may properly lead it. Sunnis are the predominant Muslim group in most countries of the world, including the United States, Europe, south Asia, and Africa. Most Muslim countries are either Sunni or Shi'a, but a few countries have significant populations of each.

These differences can lead to political tensions. In Iraq, for example, the majority of the population is Shi'a, but the country

CONTROLLING ANGER: A VIRTUE

Ḥadīth 1

عَنْ أَبِي هُرَيْرَةَ أَنَّ رَجُلاً قَالَ لِلنَّبِيِّ صَلَّى ٱللَّهُ
عَلَيْهِ وَسَلَّمَ: أَوْصِنِي، قَالَ: " لاَ تَغْضَبْ ". فَكَرَّرَ
ٱلسُّؤَالَ ثَلاَثَ مَرَّاتٍ ، وَكَرَّرَ
ٱلرَّسُولُ ٱلْجَوَابَ نَفْسَهُ .

(رَوَاهُ ٱلْبُخَارِي)

Transliteration

`An 'Abī Hurairata 'anna rajulan qāla li (a)n-Nabiyyi,
Ṣalla-(A)llāhu `alai-hi wa-Sallama, "Awṣinī": Qāla: "Lā
taghḍab" Fa-karrara (a)s-su'āla thalātha marrātin
wa-karrara (a)r-Rasūlu (a)l-jawāba nafsa-hu.
(Rawāhu Al-Bukhārī)

Translation

It was reported by 'Abū Hurairah that once a person said
to Rasūlullāh ﷺ: "Give me a piece of advice." Rasūlullāh
ﷺ replied; "Do not become angry." The man asked
repeatedly, and each time Rasūlullāh ﷺ gave the same
reply: "Do not become angry." *(Narrated by Al-
Bukhārī)*

Above is an example of hadith showing the Arabic version as well as the English
translation. (Reproduced with permission from Dr. Khalid Mahmood Shaikh, *A Study
of Hadith*, Skokie, Ill: IQRA International Educational Foundation, 1996, p. 81.)

was ruled between 1979 and 2003 by Saddam Hussein, a Sunni. Since his overthrow, unrest between the two groups has escalated. Abu Musab al-Zarqawi, a Sunni leader of Al Qaeda forces in Iraq killed by an American airstrike, had called on Sunnis to "confront the poison of the Shi'ite snakes who are afflicting you" just before his death.[7] Yet, at the same time, Sunnis and Shi'as in Detroit were attending joint gatherings in an effort to demonstrate the fundamental unity of all Muslims.[8]

Some 85 to 90 percent of all Muslims belong to the Sunni group. The name "Sunni" comes from the word Sunnah, the collection of the accepted traditions about the prophet and his companions. Sunnis believe that the first four successors to Muhammad were properly chosen. They try to follow the teachings of the prophet Muhammad and these four leaders.

The formal structure of Sunni Islamic religion is decentralized. Imams, or religious leaders, are scholars rather than priests. They usually lead Friday prayers and take the lead in administration of the mosque, but any Sunni Muslim may perform these tasks. Sunni imams are the main interpreters of Islamic law and customs for their communities. They attend religious colleges and gain respect as they lead and teach over the years. There is no one leader of the Sunni Muslims.

The remaining 10 to 15 percent, the Shi'a, feel that as Muhammad's cousin and one of his sons-in-law (and thus Muhammad's closest male relative), Ali was the rightful successor to Muhammad from the very beginning, in 632 C.E. The name Shi'a comes from the phrase "Shi'at Ali," Party of Ali. They consider the previous three leaders to have denied Ali his rightful position.

The Shi'as have a more centralized religious organization than do the Sunnis. Their legitimate religious leaders, called Imams, are believed to be divinely inspired and thus have both religious and political authority. In the most common form of Shi'a Islam, the twelfth Imam is believed to have disappeared from the earth; it is said that he will return at the end of time. In his absence, Shi'a scholars called ayatollahs (the word means "sign/word of God") make binding legal and religious interpretations, which are respected and followed by other Shi'as.

Shi'as live mainly in Iraq, much of Iran, Pakistan, and Lebanon. Shah Ismail Safavi, who ruled Iran from 1501 to 1524, made Shi'ism the official religion of his empire, with the result that most of the population became Shi'a. Within Shi'a Islam, there are several subgroups that follow different imams.

Sufis

Sufis are the mystics of Islam. They seek to experience the actual presence of God through self-denial, meditation, and love and service to others. The name "Sufi" comes from the Arabic word for wool, which describes the plain clothes the Sufis wear. They are not monks and usually marry and have families. Sufis may be Sunni or Shi'a or belong to any Muslim sect. Sufi orders, or groups, were formed in the twelfth century, although Sufi practices had existed long before then. Sufis tend to venerate saints who are founders of the Sufi orders or other pious Muslims. In the twentieth century, Sufism was banned in Saudi Arabia, where a type of Islam called Wahhabism is practiced.

Rabia al-Adawiyya, who died in 801, was a female Sufi who is said to have performed many miracles. She encouraged emotional expression and practices that demonstrated love for God. Unlike most other Sufis, she refused to marry, saying she had room in her heart only for God.

Sufi poetry is hauntingly beautiful. One of the best-known Sufi writers is Rumi, who died in 1273. Rumi's followers sometimes spin around and around while chanting the names of God. They are known as the whirling dervishes.

The prophet Muhammad gave his Farewell Sermon shortly before he died. At Arafat, the mountain many believe to be the landing place of Noah's ark, he outlined five duties all Muslims were expected to observe. These duties are usually called the "Five Pillars of Islam." All Muslims accept these five pillars as their most important obligations, although some groups interpret them differently and some add other required tasks. At its most basic level, Islam teaches that belief is nothing without action—expressing faith, doing right, and carrying out acts of worship.

The First Pillar: Shahada

Shahada is the testament of belief. Anyone who sincerely recites this is considered a Muslim. A person born to Muslim parents is assumed to be Muslim but learns to recite this testament during his or her childhood.

The Shahada consists of two parts. The first states, "I declare that there is no god but God." The belief that there is only one deity or god is called monotheism.

The second part of the testament states, "I declare that Muhammad is the messenger of God." Muhammad is not believed to be the only messenger of God. He is, however, believed to be the last prophet sent by God. Muhammad's life choices and teachings, called the Sunnah, constitute a guide for every aspect of life, in addition to the Qur'an.

When a person makes this statement of belief, she or he acknowledges that God alone deserves worship and ultimate obedience. Thus the person is known as a "submitter," or a Muslim.

The Second Pillar: Salat

Salat refers to prayer. The word literally means "connection," indicating its function in connecting human beings with God. Muslims are expected to pray five times at specified periods throughout the day. Regular practice is considered to be essential for spiritual growth and to help a person live according to the precepts of Islam. Observant Muslims take a break from their routine activities for these periods of prayer, each of which lasts about ten to fifteen minutes. The times of prayer are dawn, just after noon, the middle of the afternoon, just after the sun sets, and after dusk. In addition to the formal prayers, Muslims make voluntary prayers at other times.

Prayers do not have to be said in a mosque. Muslims may pray at home or work, or wherever they may be at the prescribed time. The worshipper should be clean, stand in a clean place, and be modestly dressed. A certain ritual for washing precedes prayer. It is thought to help wash thoughts of the outside world out of the heart and mind.

All worshippers face the direction of the Ka'aba in Mecca. Originally, the prophet Muhammad had instructed his followers to face Jerusalem as a gesture of solidarity with Judaism and Christianity as fellow monotheistic traditions. In January 624 C.E. in Medina, Muhammad received a revelation that they should face the Ka'aba when praying. Praying in the direction of the Ka'aba also symbolized a return to what Muslims believed were the origins of the Islamic faith, since the Ka'aba was believed by Muslims to have been built by Abraham for the worship of the one God.

> The prophet Muhammad outlined five duties all Muslims were expected to observe. These duties are usually called the "Five Pillars of Islam."

Muslims follow a prescribed series of movements, including bowing, kneeling, and touching the head to the floor, all conducted while reverently reciting prayers and verses of the Qur'an. Formal prayers end with the prayer for peace. Individual prayers may be said after formal prayers or at other times. All prayers except individual devotions are said in Arabic. The Qur'an is always recited in Arabic during prayers.

Although it appears that there are many rules for the formal prayers, in fact, the intent to pray honestly is considered the most important. And if a prayer time is missed, Muslims try to make it up at a later time or ask God for forgiveness.

Friday Prayers. Muhammad appointed the Friday midday prayers as a time for the community to worship together. Friday is not a holy day like the Sabbath for Jews or Sunday for Christians, but it does have a somewhat festive quality. Friday prayers, called "jumu'ah," are normally held at a mosque and draw large crowds. In addition to the usual prayers, the imam or leader of prayer gives a brief sermon, offering social and religious commentary on current events and issues and discussing how to live a lifethat is pleasing to God. In most countries, men and women pray in separate areas of the mosque, or else women form rows behind the men for reasons of modesty.

The Third Pillar: Sawm

Sawm is fasting during the month of Ramadan, a time of special spiritual striving. In Muslim countries and communities, the tenor of life changes at this time. People stay up later, take extra time off for prayers and reading the Qur'an, and turn their thoughts inward. Ramadan is the ninth month in the Islamic lunar calendar, and it lasts about thirty days. Because it is based on the sighting of the new moon and not the course of the sun, its time changes each conventional year. Lunar months are shorter than the months used in the Western calendar, which have been lengthened to bring them into alignment with the solar year. The changing time of Ramadan means that, if the month falls in the summer, Muslims must fast for many hours because the days are longer. In winter, the hours people fast are much fewer. Muslims are encouraged to fast on certain other days of the year as well.

Rules for Ramadan. All healthy adult Muslims are expected to refrain from food, water, and sexual activity while the sun is up. Smoking and chewing gum are also off-limits, as are cough drops. They may eat and drink only before sunrise and after sunset. In addition, Muslims gather to say special prayers at night and visit the sick and needy. They are also expected to make a greater effort not to fight, curse, or lie, and to cultivate positive attitudes and behaviors in response to the stress of fasting. Children do not have to fast.

During Ramadan, Muslims rise before the sun in order to eat a light breakfast called "sahoor." After breakfast, the morning prayers are said and selections from the Qur'an are read. After this time, no food or water may be consumed.

When the sun finally sets, Muslims gather to eat another small meal, called the "iftar." Typically it includes milk, dates, and water in emulation of the prophet Muhammad, who usually broke his fast with dates. Then the sunset prayer is said, at home or in the mosque if possible. After prayers, family and friends gather for a hearty meal. It is customary for special

Muslims break their Ramadan fast at their mosque in Iowa. It is the custom for special foods to be served for the evening meal during Ramadan.

dishes to be served for the evening meal during Ramadan. Even career women make time-consuming specialties for their families. Sometimes it can be very draining. One woman complained that it was like cooking Christmas dinner every day for a month![1]

After dinner, Muslims may return to the mosque for special prayers held only during Ramadan. The entire Qur'an is read in the mosque over the course of the month. The "Night of Power" marks the occurrence of the first revelation of what became the Qur'an. It is observed on the twenty-seventh night of Ramadan. Muslims stay up all night, praying and meditating during this sacred time.

Id al-Fitr. The end of Ramadan is marked by the Feast of Id al-Fitr, the "Feast of the Fast Breaking." The festivities last several days. Muslims give presents to their children and donate to charity so that less fortunate people may celebrate the end of Ramadan with new clothes and good food.

The Fourth Pillar: Zakat

Zakat refers to obligatory donations. Muhammad was very concerned with social fairness. Having grown up as an orphan, sent from home to home, he knew the pain in the life of the poor and the outcast. He was very concerned with making special provisions for dignified support to those who needed it. Muhammad also wanted people who had money and possessions not to become too attached to them. That is why these donations are called zakat, which literally means "purification." This word reminds Muslims that money belongs to God, and it can make us more attached to personal pleasures than to the good of others if it is not used properly.

Zakat consists of required contributions made by Muslims to their mosques or other charitable organizations. The general amount is 2.5 percent of one's total assets each year. The offerings are not for the mosque itself, but are distributed to the needy. A person struggling to support a family is not expected to create a hardship for the family by paying zakat. People must pay their own debts before paying zakat, and only those who have a certain amount of savings and a reasonable living standard are accountable to God for fulfilling this obligation.[2]

In a few Muslim countries, zakat takes the form of a tax collected by the government. It is not collected if paying it would cause hardship. Some Shi'a groups require that the members who are able to pay the basic zakat contribute a separate part of their earnings in addition to the annual amount. The extra money goes to support religious institutions and leaders, enabling them to remain free of governmental control.

The Fifth Pillar: Hajj

The hajj is the pilgrimage to Mecca. All Muslims who can afford to do so are expected to travel to Mecca once in their lives for the sacred pilgrimage during the month of Dhul Hijjah, the twelfth month of the Islamic lunar calendar. If people cannot afford to make the trip, they are not obligated to go. A person may not borrow money for this sacred trip; however, some governments offer financial assistance to those in need. Specialized travel agencies help Muslims make arrangements for the hajj. The government of Saudi Arabia, in which Mecca is located, works out the number of pilgrims who may arrive each year in conjunction with the countries from which the pilgrims come. Only Muslims may make the hajj.

According to Islamic tradition, the rituals of the hajj date back to the patriarch Abraham and his son Ishmael, builders of the Ka'aba. Later on, the polytheist Arabs focused their practices around the Ka'aba as well. The prophet Muhammad faithfully observed these ancient rituals, especially the custom of walking around the Ka'aba seven times, even before he began receiving the inspiration of the Qur'an. He incorporated many of the rituals into Islam. He felt that their observance would serve to unify all Muslims.

Hajj Rituals. When a pilgrim arrives at Mecca, he or she bathes at the entry station and puts on special clothing. Men may not wear anything with stitches in it; women wear simple, loose-fitting clothing. Both men and women usually wear white. Sexual relations are forbidden during the hajj, as well as cutting the hair or nails, wearing perfume, killing living things, and fighting. Interestingly, the hajj is one time when men and women are not separated. All pilgrims, regardless of gender, perform the rituals together.

Pilgrims first approach the Ka'aba, the sacred place of worship believed by Muslims to have been built by Abraham. The Ka'aba is a cube-shaped building about forty feet long on each side and fifty feet high. It is now enclosed within a huge mosque with thousands of columns and minarets. Pilgrims walk around the Ka'aba seven times, reciting certain prayers and reaching out to touch or kiss the black stone located in one of its walls.

Then pilgrims go to drink from the ancient well of Zam Zam, from which Hagar and her son Ishmael are said to have drunk after they had been cast out by Abraham at Sarah's insistence (Genesis 21:19). Next they walk back and forth between the hills of Safa and Marwa. This is where Hagar is said to have run up and down in despair, looking for water for her son and herself before finding the well.

Pilgrims then travel to Mina, a barren, open plain where millions of people assemble and spend the night in tents. The next day, they move on to the valley of Arafat and pray out in the open desert. That night, pilgrims travel to Muzdalifah and gather twenty-one small stones. When they return to Mina, the pilgrims throw the stones at three pillars said to represent Satan. Next, the pilgrims return to Mecca and, by the tenth day, complete a final seven ritual trips around the Ka'aba.

Muslims making a pilgrimage to Mecca, photographed in 1910. The Ka'aba, a box-shaped granite building, is a sacred place of worship believed to have been built by Abraham.

Pilgrims often travel to Medina and Jerusalem after the hajj. When Muslims visit Mecca and the Ka'aba outside of the hajj period, it is called the "umrah," or "Lesser Pilgimage."[3]

The huge numbers of people making the hajj pilgrimage and the great enthusiasm they share have sometimes combined with deadly results. In January 2006, over 2.5 million people were at Mina performing the stoning ritual when some pilgrims tripped and startled others. A stampede ensued and at least 345 people were trampled to death. In the past twenty years, about three thousand people have died in hajj tragedies. Saudi Arabian authorities, who have responsibility for the holy sites, have tried to make improvements in walkways and have added more security staff.[4]

Other Beliefs: Creation, Angels, Jinn, and People

The Qur'an says that God created the world in six days or stages. This account is similar to the story the book of Genesis relates. However, the Qur'an also describes stages of what scientists now call the "Big Bang" theory of creation, and makes some sophisticated suggestions regarding a theory of evolution.

God is said to have created angels, beings of light who obey only his commands, says the Qur'an: "And we [angels] descend not but by the command of thy Lord." (19:6)

According to Islam, God also made Jinn. These creatures, made from fire, can choose to obey God or not. They are some-times referred to as good or bad spirits, depending on which path they choose. As they say in the Qur'an, "some of us are good and others of us are below that." (72:11)

The creation of humans by God also echoes the Genesis story in some ways. God is said to have made humans from clay into which he breathed his spirit. Since humans have the divine breath in them, they have the capacity to choose good or evil for themselves. The idea that people could choose to do good or bad deeds was strange to the Arabs in the time of Muhammad.

They viewed human life as predestined for good or bad, a view called fatalism. The Qur'an, on the other hand, teaches that people are free to ignore the call of God and do as they wish. However, according to the first line of the Qur'an, God is all merciful. Even if a person has done bad deeds all of his or her life, a single request for forgiveness and compassion will immediately be answered by God.

The Afterlife

Most Arabs of Muhammad's time did not believe in an afterlife. The Qur'an took a very different view, which is similar to that found in Judaism and Christianity. It said that after physical death, people would arise from the sleep of the grave and face a Day of Judgment, when they would have to account for all their actions, both good and bad. At that time, they would pass on to either heaven or hell.[5]

4 Religious and Cultural Customs Among Muslims

It is difficult to identify specific social norms and customs that are uniquely "Islamic." Attitudes and activities may appear to have originated in Islam when in fact they derive from a combination of religious, cultural, and historical influences. Here we will separate customs based on the religion of Islam from practices that are not Islamic and those that existed before the establishment of Islam. We will also look at customs from different countries and regions that are often assumed to be purely Muslim but are really not.

Values and Customs Based on the Religious Teachings of Islam

Nearly all Muslims observe the five pillars of their faith. The observance of these practices gives rise to a strong feeling of shared identity among Muslims. This is called the ummah, the world community of Muslims. The ummah shares a common core of identity and interests despite the many cultural and national differences that exist among Muslims.

The mosque or "masjid" is the center of the Muslim community. In addition to community gatherings, many mosques in non-Muslim countries provide religious education on a weekend day so that the children can learn about their faith and share its practices with one another.

Local customs frequently influence how people practice their required religious duties. For instance, in many Muslim communities the Friday community prayer time is followed by a lunch gathering. Friends chat and children play. During Ramadan, the evening meals are a time when family and friends visit. Collecting money for the needy can evolve into group projects.

Muslim social activities do not include intoxicants. The Qur'an specifically forbids them. This ban includes alcohol and "recreational" drugs. (Medicinal drugs used with a doctor's prescription to treat an illness are not prohibited.) The Qur'an also prohibits any kind of gambling.

Muslim dietary laws define what Muslims may eat. Muslims are expected to eat foods that are deemed "halal," or lawful, by Islamic food laws. These rules are not unlike the kosher laws of Judaism. Animal blood, pork products, and animals that have died rather than having been slaughtered are not eaten. There are strict laws governing how food animals are killed, which ensure that the animals die painlessly and that the meat is clean.

Work practices are also covered by religious rules. Business must be conducted honestly, and receiving interest on loans is specifically forbidden. Charity is encouraged, as well as kindness to those who owe money and cannot repay because of unforeseen setbacks. All contracts and agreements must be in writing. Business that includes dealings in "haram," or forbidden items, such as liquor or pork products, is prohibited.

Taking an active role in creating a just society is a religious duty, as the Qur'an says: "You [Muslims] encourage what is right and forbid what is wrong." (3:110) Since specific verses of the Qur'an teach that religious life, communal activities, and political life are all linked, many Muslims are active in community and charity work.

How Religious Customs Become Politicized

Muslims do not make visual representations of Muhammad or any other revered figure. Islam strongly opposes the worship of idols and cautions against making Muhammad an object of worship. Muslims interpreted this to mean that they should not make representations of any humans or animals. Consequently, Muslim artists have traditionally used geometric shapes and Arabic script in their creations, especially in religious settings such as mosques. However, many artworks and crafts produced historically and today do depict human and animal figures in various ways. Indian and Persian artists portray Muhammad in some instances, but his face is shown as a flame; it is never depicted in detail.

In late 2005, some cartoons showing the prophet Muhammad were published in a Danish newspaper. These pictures have outraged many Muslims around the world. While most Muslims object to depicting the Prophet in any form, they became angry especially because in the cartoons Muhammad was associated with bombs and terrorist activities.

Many non-Muslims find the furor over these drawings hard to understand. Most European countries as well as the United States place great value on the concept of freedom of the press.

Freedom of the press means that people are allowed to write anything they want, regardless of whether their message offends others. (Even in free societies, there are certain limits on obscenity and classified information, and people can be prosecuted if what they have written is untrue or causes others harm.) Muslims may agree with the concept of a free press in general, but many feel that violating their ban on depicting the prophet Muhammad is unnecessarily offensive.[1]

Headscarves and Burkas

It is commonly thought that the Qur'an requires all Muslim women to cover their hair with a scarf or to conceal their bodies entirely in a large, shapeless garment called a burka. This is a common interpretation of the Qur'an, but it is not the only one. The subject is somewhat complex.

Muslim women and men in Muhammad's day were expected to dress modestly. The Qur'an does make one specific reference to women covering their upper bodies: "Let them (women) wear their head-coverings over their bosoms." (24:31) Some scholars have argued that the head-covering mentioned by the Qur'an was a long scarf worn by aristocratic Persian and Byzantine women of the time. It was worn for reasons of fashion, not modesty. And the part of the body that the Qur'an says to cover is not the head or hair but the chest. These scholars suggest that when Muslims began settling in the conquered territories and mingling with other cultures, they adopted this long scarf and gave it a religious significance. Those who could afford them eagerly adopted the practice.[2]

Another verse of the Qur'an has been interpreted to mean that women should cover themselves completely when in the presence of non-family members: "And when you ask of them any goods, ask of them from behind a curtain." (33:53) However, some scholars say that this verse actually addresses a problem that was apparently occurring in Muhammad's household in Medina. People were eager to visit with Muhammad and would come uninvited into his home. The whole verse lays down rules of good behavior for visiting not only Muhammad's home, but anyone's.

Today, some sort of head or body covering has become a nearly universal mark of a devout Muslim woman. In some

A four-year-old girl in the Middle Eastern country of Bahrain protests against the French government's ban on the headscarf, or hijab. Her Arabic sign reads, "Hijab is the symbol of our pride."

countries such as Saudi Arabia they are required, but in other places many women wear headscarves by choice. In fact, some teenage Muslim girls in the United States and Europe want to wear headscarves even when their parents do not expect or want them to. Some adult women who never wore the headscarf have changed their minds and now wear it.[3] Yet in other countries, such as Iraq, women who leave their homes without headscarves may be harassed or even punished by armed men seeking to enforce their own standards of appropriate dress.[4]

Are Most Muslims Arabs?

Because Arabic is the language of the Qur'an and because many Arabic countries are Muslim, it is a common and quite natural assumption that most, if not all, Muslims are Arabs. An "Arab" is a person who speaks a dialect of Arabic as a native language and who regards him or herself as an Arab.[5] In fact, most Muslims are not Arabs. Between 10 and 20 percent of the Muslims in the world were born in Arab countries.[6] About 20 percent of Arab Americans are Muslim.[7]

It is possible to make some broad observations about Arab culture, as long as we bear in mind that generalizations do not apply to every single individual Arab. Like many other cultures, Arab society tends to hold on to traditional values, such as the importance of the family, the different roles that men and women play in the home and in society, and the wisdom that elders possess. Religion, whether Islam or another, is very important in most Arab societies.[8]

Arabs may be Muslims or Christians, or they may follow some other religion. Eighteen countries are wholly or partly members of the Arab world: Algeria, Bahrain, Egypt, Iraq, Jordan, Kuwait, Lebanon, Libya, Morocco, Oman, Qatar, Saudi Arabia, Sudan, Syria, Tunisia, the United Arab Emirates, Yemen, and the region of Palestine. Iran is not an Arab country, and Iranians speak the Persian language and have their own distinctive culture. However, the population of Iran is almost completely Muslim. Indonesia, Afghanistan, and Pakistan are also non-Arab countries whose populations are mostly Muslim.

Pre-Islamic Customs in Arabia

A substantial portion of what may appear to be Islamic social norms are in fact customs that existed in the Arabian peninsula and Middle East before Islam. Since Islam originated in Arabia, many traces of that earlier society are embedded in the religion. The time before the revelations to Muhammad is called "jahiliyah." Many verses of the Qur'an speak to the conditions of the times: war, the importance of family and clans, the status of women, and the power of the spoken word. Islam has also incorporated some early Arabian religious rituals, such as the rituals of the hajj.

Clans. The harsh conditions of desert living demanded that people give absolute loyalty to certain people whom they could trust to preserve their lives. Thus the institution of the tribe or clan was born. Each clan took care of its members. The existence of the group was most important. Hence each clan kept together and did not trust other clans. Any offense against one member of the clan was viewed as an offense against all. Death was the usual punishment for an insult against one's clan. Sometimes these punishments took the form of vendettas, or murders of several people for each loss the tribe had suffered. Muhammad outlawed vendettas when he moved to Medina.

The Arabs had to stay on the move so that their animals could find food. This nomadic existence resulted in the Arabs of Muhammad's time being very independent. Each tribe had a leader called a "shaykh," the forerunner of the modern word sheik. This person, always a man, was chosen by the clan to lead it, but he did not have absolute power. He took care of the poor in the clan, offered hospitality to strangers, and maintained order in the group. His most important duty was leading his clan into battle.[9] The great accomplishment of Islam was the unification of these independent clans into one cohesive group, united not by their allegiance to a political leader but by their belief in one god.

War. In seventh-century Arabia, clans routinely raided each other's store of goods and animals when necessary for survival. If a member of one clan killed a member of another, the clan of the victim would try to kill several members of the murderer's clan. The Qur'anic verses said to have been given to Muhammad after he moved to Medina put limits on what kinds of wars could be fought and how one should behave during and after battles. These verses lead some readers of the Qur'an to assume that Islam is a religion of war. For instance, religious historian and author Richard Connerney believes that "the fact of Muslim military might is the rock on which the entire community of the faithful is erected.... It is an original state of political and military strength that promotes the religious message."[10] However, others argue that the Qur'an's military advice was intended for the people and conditions of Muhammad's own time, and it was intended to decrease wars, not increase them. Muslims were prohibited from harming non-combatants, including women, children, and the elderly. They were also not to attack places of worship or to burn down trees or crops. Such regulations put severe limits on Muslims in relation to the practices of the time. Most importantly, Muslims are instructed in the Qur'an not to be the aggressors but only to defend themselves, and if the enemy seeks peace, to make peace. Many Muslims point out that terrorists who cite the Qur'an as justification for their actions

A substantial portion of what may appear to be Islamic social norms are in fact customs that existed in the Arabian peninsula and Middle East before Islam.

ignore the limits that the book places on battle. Most Muslims state that those who believe the terrorists' justification do not understand the whole message of the Qur'an.[11]

Local Customs Among Muslims

Many non-Arab countries have substantial Muslim populations. Customs from these countries get mixed in with Islamic practices, creating a unique blend. Some regional traditions are incorrectly identified as Islamic by outsiders.

Africa. Sufis, the Muslim mystics, were active in spreading Islam in Africa. Sufis were more willing than more orthodox Muslims to accept local religious customs and blend them with

A student in Mali checks his writing against a worn copy of the Qur'an. Islam is a major religion in many African countries.

Islamic practices. This willingness helped them spread Islam in Africa and Asia, where devotion to saints and magic were deeply rooted.

The Berbers were already well established in North Africa when the Muslim Arabs conquered the region in the seventh century. Islam took root quickly in this area, which now consists of the countries of Libya, Algeria, Tunisia, and Morocco. But the Berber culture never died out. The Berbers traditionally worshipped saints and marabouts. Marabouts are wise men, living and dead, who are thought to have a special connection with God.

South of the Berber territory in Africa is the country called Sudan. The northern part of Sudan is Muslim. The Sudanese, like the Berbers, have mingled some of their native beliefs with Islam. They celebrate non-Islamic harvest rites. They pray to saints, especially in times of illness, with great fervor. They also hold large festivals on the holy days of popular saints. Imams are asked to write verses of the Qur'an or magical sayings which are then used to ward off evil and bring on healing.[12]

South Asia. In Indonesia, Muslims have long practiced their religion with rites that recall the island's Hindu and polytheistic past. In the annual Labuhan ceremony, silk, bananas, curry, and hair and toenail clippings are thrown into the sea in honor of the goddess of the seas. Those doing the throwing are Muslims. They take pride in preserving their local rituals while still remaining devout followers of Islam. There is a tendency to share some diverse practices; for example, Sunni Muslims often participate in the Shi'a commemoration of Ashura.[13] Ashura commemorates the death of Muhammad's grandson Hussein in 680 C.E. at Karbala. This was the first serious battle between what became the Sunni and Shi'a branches of Islam.

Pashtunistan. The mountainous area that covers eastern Afghanistan and northwestern Pakistan is home to a group of people called Pashtuns. They are mostly Sunni Muslims, but their history is much older than Islam. Over many generations, the rugged, mountainous geography of this area created fierce, independent people called Pashtuns, known for their hospitality, loyalty, and love of family. They are quite willing to fight on behalf of their tribes and their beliefs. Their strong tribal organization enabled them to repel the invasion of Alexander the Great in 327 B.C.E. Centuries later, the Soviet Union got a taste of Pashtun independence when it invaded Afghanistan in December of 1979. The Soviet Union was seeking control of a port on the Indian Ocean to increase its ability to trade, and Afghanistan was the first step in that direction. After ten weary years of fighting, the Soviets were forced to withdraw in defeat.

The Pashtuns live by a strict code of honor. They feel that wrongs done to one member of the tribe must be avenged. However, the revenge is not always violent. Death may be avenged by a marriage between the families of the killer and the victim. The Pashtuns are renowned for their hospitality, and they take the role of hosting a guest very seriously. One reporter was surprised to find that when he visited several fierce warlords, he was first expected to share tea and pastries before getting to the interview.[14]

Although many members of the Taliban, a group that ruled Afghanistan from 1996 to 2001 and instituted a very strict form of Islamic law, were Pashtuns, the Pashtuns as a whole have never approved of this militant form of religion.[15]

Turkey. Turkey was the seat of the Ottoman Empire from 1280 to 1922 C.E. The empire was wealthy and cosmopolitan for much of this time. Turkey's contact with many different cultures has given it a comfort level with foreign ideas. Many wealthy Turks in medieval times had their pictures painted by

Western artists. The man who seized Constantinople from the Christians in 1453 and renamed it Istanbul, Sultan Mehmed II, had his portrait painted by the Venetian painter Gentile Bellini in 1480, reflecting changes in court culture in response to contact with Europeans.[16] After World War I, the empire was dismantled by European powers and Turkey became an independent nation led by Mustafa Kemal, who established one of the most secular governments in the Middle East, despite the fact that over 98 percent of the population is Muslim.

Today, the cities of Turkey are intellectually liberal, culturally sophisticated places. Istanbul boasts a nightlife that rivals that of any Western city. In the small villages, however, it is a different story. Most inhabitants of small towns live in extreme poverty. Periodically, ethnic minorities are persecuted. Turkish national identity is promoted, and religion continues to play an important and frequently controversial role in society. Clashes between those who wish to impose a stricter form of Islamic law and those who want Turkey to retain its officially secular position are frequent and sometimes deadly.[17]

Within Turkey live many Kurds, a semi-nomadic people who inhabit the eastern part of the country as well as northern Iraq and northwest Iran. Approximately 15 million people are in this group. They are Muslims but not Arabs. Many belong to the ʿAlawi sect of Islam, neither Sunni nor Shiʿa. They have their own holy days, prayers, and religious activities. The Kurds have battled with the governments of Turkey, Iran, and Iraq since 1920 to have an independent country of their own. They launched terrorist attacks in Turkey in the 1980s in support of their goals. The Turkish government has responded with great force to these attacks, and has not given in to Kurdish demands for self-government. The Kurdish language and ethnic customs are officially banned, but the Kurds continue to seek autonomy and representation.

5 Women and Islam

Non-Muslim Americans have many questions about the status of Muslim women. Does Islamic law permit a man to marry four wives? Why would a woman agree to be just one of several wives? Can women work outside the home? Can they drive? Can they divorce their husbands? Can they be divorced without their consent? Do they inherit and control property?

The answers to these questions are complex. In many Muslim countries, women possess some legal rights, but social and cultural pressures may prevent them from exercising them. In non-Muslim countries, individual Muslim women and families, depending on their social and economic positions, may feel free to abide by or disregard the wishes of the Muslim community.

In Arabia at the time of Muhammad's birth, women were considered to be essentially the property of their fathers until they married. At that time they became the property of their husbands. Men could take as many wives as they wished. When a man died, his son "inherited" his father's wives as his own. In this society, girl babies were sometimes killed because they were not as useful to the clan as boys. This situation, when men are in charge of society, is called patriarchy. The inequalities it created are the reason why many verses of the Qur'an address the topic of the status of women. Some verses of the Qur'an reflect the old patriarchal view of the status of women, but others actually give far-reaching rights to women in matters of marriage, ownership of property, and personal freedom. Although the new customs proposed by the Qur'an may appear outmoded today, they were revolutionary at the time.

How Did Muhammad Treat Women?

Muhammad and his first wife, Khadija, were married for twenty-four years. Although local custom gave Muhammad the right to marry other women, Khadija remained his only wife. About a year after Khadija died, Muhammad married Sawdah, a widow who could help raise Muhammad's young children and provide support to him. At the same time, Abu Bakir, Muhammad's faithful follower, offered him his daughter A'isha in marriage, and Muhammad accepted. A'isha was only six years old at the time, and the couple did not live together until later. Muhammad ultimately married thirteen women after Khadija's death. All but A'isha were widows or divorcees. Some of the marriages helped forge political alliances with tribes outside Medina.

Many hadith say that Muhammad strongly disapproved of wife beating, which was apparently common at the time. He said about men who strike their wives that "you will not find these men as the best among you." In another place he is quoted as saying, "the best of you is he who is best to his wife."[1] The stories about Muhammad's personal life make it clear that he honored and cherished women. He is said to have done his own shopping, cleaning, and cooking. He mended his own clothes.[2]

The women in Muhammad's life were strong individuals who helped him spread the message of Islam even in difficult circumstances. Khadija supported Muhammad without hesitation when he first heard the words of the Qur'an, and she continued to do so when the message he preached caused turmoil and brought danger to the family. A'isha also provided the emotional support that Muhammad needed, and did not hesitate to criticize him when he did something that annoyed her or others. Through his personal life, Muhammad showed his followers that women should not be treated like possessions, as the Arabs were doing. They deserved respect and legal rights.

> **Some verses of the Qur'an give far-reaching rights to women in matters of marriage, ownership of property, and personal freedom.**

The Qur'an on Marriage

Polygamy was a common pre-modern practice in many cultures, including Arabia before Islam. There were no restrictions on the number of wives a man could marry and no legal obligations for men to take care of their families. The Qur'an imposes a limit of four wives per man, and it also says that a man must not marry more than one woman unless he can care for and provide for his wives equally. Today, most Muslims see monogamy as the norm.

The Qur'an issued important new laws concerning marriage that improved women's financial status, both within the marriage and in the event that it failed. Arabic marriage customs required that a woman receive a dowry upon marriage. In some cultures, women receive property, called a dowry, from their own family or the family of their husbands, when they are married. In Muhammad's time, the husband gave a dowry to the wife, which the woman's family usually kept (and usually spent). The Qur'an decreed that women were to keep their dowries for themselves. Working women were also allowed to keep any money they earned, instead of having to give it to their husbands or families. These Qur'anic guidelines are usually followed today, even in instances when the wife's family has provided the dowry and the husband's family has retained it.

Divorce in the Qur'an

The Qur'an introduced another new procedure. Formerly, only men had been allowed to divorce their wives. Now women could initiate divorce. This does not mean that the Qur'an was encouraging marriages to be dissolved. Muhammad is reported to have said, "Of all the permitted things, divorce is the most abominable with God."[3] The change was a matter of recognizing the reality that women might want to end a marriage for legitimate reasons. Although in most Muslim cultures, the process often favored the husband in economic and practical terms, Islam's stance on divorce still constituted an improvement in the lives of women at the time. Remarriage after divorce was permitted for both men and women.

Sura 4:35 describes the Qur'anic procedure for divorce: "And if you fear a breach between the two [husband and wife], appoint an arbiter from his people and an arbiter from her people." This means that a judge appoints a member of each person's family to investigate the situation in the marriage. The judge listens to the reports from both arbiters and tries to help the husband and wife reconcile their differences. If this is not possible, the judge helps determine the terms of the divorce settlement.[4]

However, other Qur'anic verses show that an alternative procedure for divorce also existed. Traditionally in Arabia, a man could obtain a "temporary divorce" simply by saying "talaq" to his wife, which means "to be left free." He did not have to give a reason for wanting to end the marriage. If the husband remained separated from his wife for three months, the divorce became final. The Qur'an left this old custom in place but added important new details. A man had to utter the "talaq" on three separate occasions, and the woman had to be allowed to take her entire dowry with her, plus her own assets and property. If there had been no dowry, the husband was obliged to make financial provision for his ex-wife. Also, a man had to pay some form of child support to his former wife if he did not decide to raise the children. These requirements made divorce financially unattractive to all but the very wealthy, and forced men to take their obligations of marriage more seriously than in the pre-Islamic era.

In Muslim countries today, divorce laws are complicated and vary widely. In some Muslim countries, the old "temporary divorce" method still exists for men. A woman wishing to end her marriage, however, has to negotiate a more complicated procedure. She must file papers with a religious or civil court, or with a recognized religious scholar. She must give a reason for wishing to leave her husband. If her reason is accepted, the divorce is final after three months. Men are usually granted custody of children over the age of two.[5]

Some Muslim countries do not allow women to divorce their husbands, despite the Qur'an's authority. Other countries require the wife to give part of her dowry to her husband, although the Qur'an says that she should keep it all. The amount she gives depends on the reason she wants to leave her husband.[6]

Other Statements in the Qur'an on Women

When Muhammad was a young man, women had no right to inherit anything from their parents or other relatives. All property passed to male relatives. The Qur'an changed this and made it clear that women were allowed to inherit from their parents and other family members. Their share was not as large as that of a male relative, however.

The Qur'an allows women to be witnesses in trials, but cautions, "Call in two male witnesses from among you, but if two men cannot be found, then one man and two women to act as witnesses." (2:282) Although some observers see this as a sign that Islam considers women inferior to men, and some Muslim cultures have taken this verse as a literal statement of gender value, some Muslims see this as a reflection of the patriarchal expectations and social reality of the time, in which women played limited roles in the public sphere.

In the harsh world of the Arabian desert, female babies had been seen as extra mouths to feed and not more help for the family. Many female infants were killed shortly after being born. The Qur'an harshly condemned and outlawed this practice: "Kill not your children for fear of poverty." (17:31)

Interestingly, the Qur'an says that women are able to receive divine revelations just as men do. However, none of the prophets were female. Because of this fact, women are still not accepted as prayer leaders when both genders are present.[7]

Cultural Concepts of the Status of Women

Despite the nearly equal status that the Qur'an and the hadith give to men and women, the actual scope of activities of Muslim women varies from country to country, and even from region to region within some countries. Cultural as well as religious factors play big roles. It is not uncommon for the cultural norms to override the religious rules. In most Muslim countries, the family, rather than the individual, is the basic and most important unit. Therefore, women are usually expected to behave in a way that preserves the existence and the good name of the family.

Comparing Women's Lives in Turkey and Saudi Arabia. Laws pertaining to the legal rights of women vary widely between Muslim countries. Two countries, Turkey and Saudi Arabia, show the extreme range of diversity in these laws.

Rights for women differ widely in Muslim countries. These women are voting in Turkey, which has a majority Muslim population but a secular government.

Turkey is a Muslim country, but prides itself on its secular (non-religious) laws. The laws allow women to vote, to travel in public without a male escort, and to make independent decisions about dress and lifestyle. Indeed, Turkey elected a female prime minister, Tansu Ciller, in 1993. However, these laws are followed mostly in the larger cities and among more educated and affluent groups. In villages and in the poorer neighborhoods of Istanbul, people follow more traditional tribal patterns of life. Women wear headscarves, and they do not travel beyond the village without male guardians. When village families move into cities, they may feel more threatened by urban life and interaction with unfamiliar people, and women may be "virtually incarcerated" in their homes by relatives who follow traditional tribal customs.[8]

Even in cosmopolitan Istanbul, old traditions can hold sway. The wife of a member of the Turkish parliament made headlines when she called the police and reported that her husband had beaten her. She allowed newspapers to print pictures of her bruises. Her husband has not been punished.[9]

Saudi Arabia is a Muslim country that follows a uniquely strict interpretation of Islamic law called Wahhabism. Women in Saudi Arabia may not associate with men who do not belong to their immediate family. They cannot vote, are forbidden to drive, and can only leave their homes with a male guardian. They must be veiled and covered from head to toe. These rules are enforced by religious policemen called mutaween. Not surprisingly, very few women work in Saudi Arabia, although some own businesses and property. Women account for over half of the university graduates in the country, but make up less than 5 percent of the workforce. The Saudi government is addressing this low level of employment by creating women-only work projects.[10]

Wife abuse in Saudi Arabia is not uncommon. Rania al-Baz, the first Saudi female broadcaster, was beaten nearly to death by her husband in 2004. Although she received much sympathy from the public, no laws were changed as a result of her experience. She bowed to pressure from her family and an Islamic judge and forgave her husband.[11]

Saudi Arabia is ruled by an absolute monarch from the Saudi royal family. Many of the king's relatives hold positions of power. There is no elected national body of representatives, and no political parties are allowed. In 2005, elections for city council members were held for the first time. Billboards went up all over the country saying, "Your voice will not be heard unless you register." Even prisoners being held in jail were allowed to vote. However, one group was not included. As one writer, a university professor, said about not being allowed to vote, "My crime is too unforgivable. My handicap is beyond help. I am a woman."[12]

Women in Other Muslim Countries. The range of opportunities for women to hold jobs and make decisions for themselves in Muslim countries varies greatly. Pakistan is an officially Muslim country. It granted women the right to vote when it became a country in 1947, and elected a woman, Benazir Bhutto, to the position of prime minister in 1988 and 1993. Women have been able to vote in some Muslim countries for many years: 1949 in the Syrian Arab Republic, 1956 in Egypt, 1962 in Algeria, 1963 in Afghanistan and Iran, 1973 in Bahrain, and 1974 in Jordan. These dates become significant when we remember that women were not allowed to vote in France until 1944. Women in Kuwait obtained the right to vote and run for office in national and local elections beginning in 2007. This was the first time women were able to vote in that country.[13]

Shirin Ebadi, an Iranian, won the Nobel Peace Prize in 2003. She is the first Muslim woman to win this award. She graduated from Tehran University in Iran. She became a lawyer and rose to become the president of the Tehran city court in 1975. In 1979 the Islamic Republic of Iran was formed. She was forced to resign because the new government did not consider women able to fill positions of leadership. She has argued forcefully for the integration of Islamic ideas with democracy in Muslim countries, and for dialogue between Western countries and developing nations.[14]

Sodaba Rasooli is a twenty-year-old engineering student at the Polytechnic University in Kabul, Afghanistan. She and other women students try to stay together on campus, both in and out of classes. If they are alone, male students tease and even abuse them. The men tell them that "girls" should not study engineering.[15]

Arranged Marriages

Marriage is viewed by the Qur'an as a contract, not as a religious sacrament. In other words, marriage requires voluntary agreement between two parties. Therefore, according to Islamic law, no one can be compelled to marry anyone without his or her consent. However, arranged marriages, whereby families choose spouses for their children, were an important piece of the social code of Arabia during Muhammad's lifetime. Such marriages are still common in many parts of the world, including many countries that happen to be Muslim. In societies that value the extended family, marriage ties are seen as uniting not just the husband and wife but also their many relatives. Therefore, an individual may come under a great deal of pressure to marry someone because of benefits the parents or other relatives think the marriage will bring to the whole family.

No verses of the Qur'an or stories from the hadith require or even encourage men or women to marry against their will. In fact, one story about Muhammad relates that a woman came to him and complained that she had been forced to marry against her will. After hearing her description of events, Muhammad annulled her marriage on the spot.[16]

Honor Killings

The status or honor of the family, including the extended family, is of primary importance in many societies. In Muslim culture, family honor is often given precedence over the status or feelings of the individual. This custom arose out of tribal practices before Islam, when a strong family was the only way to ensure an individual's survival. One common effect of this point of view is less freedom and rights for individuals in the society. The Qur'an maintained an emphasis on the value of the family.

Women in Pakistan rally to condemn an honor killing. In some societies— including Muslim and non-Muslim groups—women can be put to death for disgracing their families.

The Qur'an cautions men and women about intermingling in social situations to avoid inappropriate behavior. In many Muslim cultures, for example, men and women celebrate separately at weddings and other events, though there is often not strict segregation. Over the centuries, many Muslim scholars, who make decisions about whether a certain kind of behavior is allowed by the Qur'an and the Sunnah, have argued that men cannot resist the temptation women pose, so women and men must have their own spheres of activity. In patriarchal cultures, this has usually meant that women have been seen as a potential source of societal discord and women's activities have been restricted.[17] As a result of this thinking, women often receive the bulk of the blame whenever inappropriate behavior is suspected. For instance, if an unmarried and unrelated man and woman are seen in close company, the woman may be faulted for enticing the man. Some families go so far as to punish the woman, not the man, when a female member is sexually molested or raped.

When a woman is suspected of engaging in sex outside of marriage, she is seen as bringing shame to her family, and in some cultures, a member of the family takes it upon himself to punish the woman. Sometimes the death of the woman is considered to be an appropriate punishment to remove the family's collective sense of shame. This is known as "honor killing."

Honor killings are more frequent in isolated, rural areas. In tribal areas of Afghanistan and Pakistan, a woman may be murdered if she is thought to have disgraced her family in any way.[18] In eastern Pakistan, a twenty-five-year-old woman died after her stepfather slit her throat because the woman's husband claimed she had committed adultery. Neighbors told police she left home because her husband had abused her. Her stepfather then made sure that his family would not be further dishonored by killing his three daughters, ages eight, seven, and four. His only regret was that he was not able to kill his stepdaughter's alleged lover and set fire to his house.[19] The four girls are just part of a thousand women and girls estimated to die in Pakistan each year as the result of "honor killing."[20]

The United Nations Commission on Human Rights has documented honor killings in Bangladesh, Great Britain, Brazil, Ecuador, Egypt, India, Israel, Italy, Jordan, Morocco, Sweden, Turkey, and Uganda, in addition to Pakistan. Reports of such murders have also come in from Iraq and Iran. They occur to women belonging to various religions. They are not always committed by men. Women have killed female relatives to defend their family honor.[21] Many of these killings go unreported. Sometimes a woman's death is reported as a suicide when it was really a murder by relatives committed because of "family honor."[22]

Even when living outside of countries with traditional tribal social rules, family members may kill female relatives who are suspected of shaming the family. Six Muslim women were killed in Berlin, Germany, in early 2005 by their families because they were felt to have become too "Western." British police report an average of four complaints a week by women who fear they will be targets of honor killings.[23] Interestingly, it has become common in various countries for Muslim fathers who wish their daughters to die for an offense to ask the younger sons to commit the murder, because minors receive lighter punishments from the civil authorities.[24]

There is growing awareness of this problem in the societies in which these acts occur, and there is increasing pressure on authorities to punish the perpetrators of honor killings. Muslim organizations around the world have taken stands against this practice by declaring it to be "un-Islamic." Yet there is no apparent decrease in the numbers of women who die in this way.

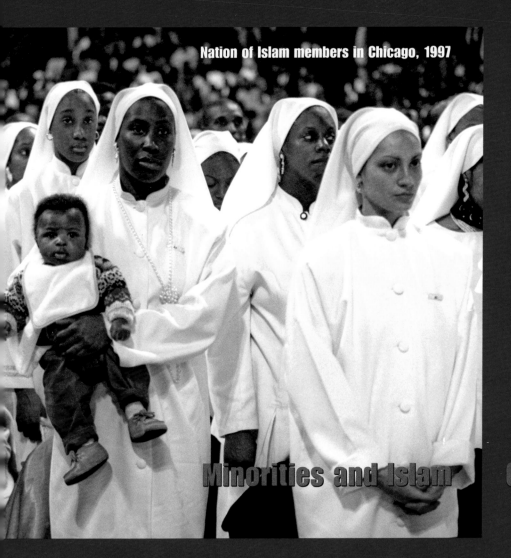

Minorities and Islam 6

About one fourth of all Muslims—a quarter of a billion people—
live in countries where they are in the minority. Almost all try
to maintain their religious practices and raise their children in
their faith while being good citizens of the countries in which
they live. Despite their large numbers, however, they frequently
face suspicion and discrimination, even in countries that pride
themselves on their tolerant, modern environment. One particularly terrible example of this discrimination in a modern
country occurred in the former country of Yugoslavia. The
Serbian majority practiced what was called "ethnic cleansing,"

killing Muslims as well as Roman Catholics in Bosnia and Kosovo.

Islam in the United States

Accurate estimates of the number of Muslims in the United States are difficult to come by. Most suggest that there are between 5 million and 7 million. This constitutes one half of one percent of the total population of the United States.[1] Approximately one fourth of all American Muslims are African American. As many as 135,000 Americans convert to Islam each year. Over half of these new converts are women.[2] Surveys asking Americans what religion they follow indicated a 109 percent increase between 1990 and 2001 in the number of people who said they were Muslim. In 2001 there were over twelve hundred mosques in the United States for regular Friday worship, an increase of 25 percent since 1995.[3]

Thirty-six percent of today's American Muslims were born in the United States, according to a recent survey. This is the fastest growing group of Muslims in the United States. Most members of this younger generation are trying to live in the American mainstream while holding on to their religious iden-tity. One way they do this is by separating the religious teachings of Islam from the cultural traditions that their parents and grandparents brought from their homelands. They seek to practice Islam in a way that seems appropriate to them in the context of American society.[4]

Origins of Islam in the United States. Muslims probably came first to the Americas in the early 1500s as unwilling par-ticipants in the African slave trade. Islam had reached North Africa within thirty years of the death of Muhammad, and it continued to spread in Africa for many centuries. When the European slave traders captured Africans to send to the New World, as many as 20 percent of the Africans were Muslims.

When the slaves arrived in the New World, they were usually forcibly converted to Christianity, and made to work under harsh conditions. Some Africans were able to pass down knowledge of Arabic and the Qur'an to their children secretly, but the connection with Islam grew dim in the face of heavy pressure from slave owners. It is possible that some Spanish and Portuguese Muslims who had hidden their true faith after being conquered in 1492 also moved to the New World.[5]

A large number of Muslim Arabs moved to the United States and Canada in the late 1800s. After the state of Israel was created in 1948, many Muslim Palestinians who were displaced from their homes moved west. The U.S. Immigration Act of 1965 enabled many people from developing nations, including Muslims, to come to the United States. Generally speaking, these groups of Muslims were able to live undisturbed and to practice their religion without fear. However, events on the world stage and ignorance among some Westerners have created challenges to Muslim integration in Western societies. The Iranian revolution in 1979, airplane hijackings by Muslim militants, and other world events, especially September 11, have made the American mainstream more aware of Muslims and, unfortunately, more afraid.

About one fourth of all Muslims—a quarter of a billion people—live in countries where they are in the minority.

Muslims in the United States, like other people of faith, also struggle to maintain their religious practices while sharing in a secular democratic society and participating in American culture and lifestyle. They must decide if they want to "look Muslim" or blend in with everyone else. For many years, Muslim leaders advised their followers to leave their scarves and other identifying markers at home. Now, many young Muslims are disregarding that advice. In North Carolina, Imani Abdul-Haqq recently started a Muslim sorority at Guilford College. She and the other members do not drink alcohol or attend co-ed parties, but they do participate in sorority and fraternity events as much as they feel is compatible with their Muslim beliefs. As Abdul-Haqq says, "I can have fun and be Muslim."[6] Shortly after September 11, a group of Muslim students in Palos Verdes, California, revived the Muslim Student Union at their high school in order to talk and pray together.[7]

Muslim parents make special efforts to teach their children the religious customs of Islam. As an example, elementary school students in the Detroit Muslim American Youth Academy reenact the pilgrimage to Mecca, called the hajj, every year. Dressed in pilgrim white, the students make the ritual seven trips around a black cube-shaped structure built to resemble the Ka'aba. Then they throw crumpled pieces of foil at three tall posts, simulating the pebbles that the hajj pilgrims throw at the three pillars in Mina.

These reenactments of a Muslim custom are not necessary in predominantly Muslim countries, where everyone is familiar with them. They have sprung up in other areas as parents teach their American-born children the customs of their faith.[8]

Three young black American men have formed a Muslim rap group called Native Deen. ("Deen" is Arabic for "way of life.") They use only percussion instruments in their performances, not wind or string instruments, which some Muslims believe Muhammad discouraged.[9]

African-American Muslims. More than one million African Americans in the United States follow Islam today.[10] This is a larger proportion than that in the general United States population. Why are African Americans attracted to Islam?

The Qur'an teaches that all people are equal before God, regardless of color. This teaching is especially attractive to those whose skin color has brought them discrimination and harassment. The hadith record that Muhammad said there was no superiority of anyone over another because of the color of his or her skin.[11]

In the early twentieth century, due to ongoing racist and segregationist practices in American society, some African Americans began looking back at their African heritage for a sense of dignity and inspiration. They rediscovered the Islamic religion that had existed in Africa when their ancestors had been captured and forced to move to the New World. They wanted to reclaim their heritage and free themselves from a religion that they felt had been used to oppress them.

At this time, several African Americans began teaching religious ideas that included some Islamic precepts. In the 1930s a man named Wallace D. Fard began preaching to people in Detroit, calling African Americans the "lost tribe of Shabazz." Little is known about Fard. He may have been born in Turkey or Iraq. Fard preached a mixed Islamic-Christian religion combined with a strong message endorsing black pride and racial separation. In 1933 he founded a group called the Nation of Islam, and in 1934 he mysteriously disappeared.

His best known follower was Elijah Muhammad. Elijah Muhammad continued preaching the Nation of Islam's message of the need for the black and white races to separate. The ideas and practices of the Nation of Islam did not conform to those of mainstream Islam. For example, Elijah Muhammad was seen as a prophet by his twentieth-century followers, whereas traditional Islam holds that there can be no prophet after Muhammad died in 632 C.E. When Elijah Muhammad died in 1975, his son, Warith Deen Muhammad, made important changes. He felt that racial hatred did not help to cure racial inequalities in the United States, and abandoned the doctrine of separation of black and white. He also led his group toward more traditional Muslim beliefs and rituals. Today, most black Muslims belong to mainstream Muslim communities.

Another important follower of Elijah Muhammad was

Malcolm X. Born Malcolm Little, Malcolm X lost his minister father in an unexplained accident when Malcolm was only six years old. His mother was left to raise eight children on her own. Eventually Malcolm turned to a life of theft and drugs to earn money for his family and deaden the pain that he felt. He landed in prison, and there learned about the teachings of Elijah Muhammad. He became a vocal minister for the Nation of Islam after he was released from prison. He eventually broke with Elijah Muhammad, but always credited him with bringing him the teachings of Islam that changed his life for the better.

Malcolm X made a pilgrimage to Mecca that affected him greatly. After his hajj, he said he had had a revelation that racial discrimination was not part of God's plan, and he adopted a more mainstream understanding of Islam. Shortly after he returned to the United States and renounced racism, Malcolm X was assassinated. The date was February 21, 1965—less than a year after he separated himself from the Nation of Islam.[12]

Malcom X, photographed in 1964, the year before he was assassinated.

Louis Farrakhan, another close associate of Elijah Muhammad, was unhappy with Warith's changes and started his own branch of the Nation of Islam. It is now the only remnant of Elijah Muhammad's original teachings. He continues to preach a doctrine of racial separation and non-traditional Islamic practices. About twenty thousand people belong to the Nation of Islam today. Farrakhan started the Million Man March in 1995, a march by African-American men in Washington, D.C., to increase voting, participation, and activism to shape American domestic policies. This march, now called the Millions More March, takes place each year, with hundreds of thousands of participants, including prominent politicians. It is no longer limited to men.

Muslims in Europe. Muslims have lived in eastern and western Europe for centuries. They ruled parts of Spain as well as southern Italy and France from the eighth century to 1492. The immense influence of the Muslims in this area is apparent in the many beautiful buildings, which are often called "Moorish." After that time, they were persecuted and driven out. Most fled to North Africa.

Many Muslim countries that had been previously ruled by European powers achieved independence in the nineteenth and twentieth centuries. Because these colonies were mostly poor, many of their citizens moved to France, Germany, and Great Britain in search of better lives. They built mosques and practiced Islam in their new countries. The inhabitants of their new lands did not always understand the immigrants' customs and religious practices. The Muslims, in turn, encountered new customs and did not find the kind of family-centered social structure that they were used to. In many European countries, violence has occurred between Muslims and non-Muslims as the tensions between the two groups have grown stronger. Some Europeans fear that the Muslim immigrants are taking jobs away from people already in the country, even though the Europeans initially welcomed the immigrants to provide labor and boost their economic situation. Muslims in Europe find that they are constantly under suspicion of being terrorists simply because they are different. Some Muslims feel they are the victims of a growing racist attitude against them.[13]

Afghanistan's chief justice, Fazel Hadi Shinwari

7

Shari'a: Religious Law

Islamic law is called "shari'a." This term is commonly misunderstood. The word itself simply means "straight path" or "right path." It can be used to ask directions (shari'a) to a place. Usually, however, shari'a refers to religious laws and social norms. Shari'a strives to provide a complete code for proper behavior in every aspect of a Muslim's life, including both individual and social levels. Islam does not separate religious practice from social or political actions. The basis of Islamic law is the Qur'an and the hadith along with the collected opinions of the companions of the prophet Muhammad. Shari'a covers areas that most Western and some Muslim countries administer under the heading of civil law, such as marriage, divorce, and inheritance. It also lays down rules for handling criminal acts such as theft and murder. The process of arriving at legal interpretations in Islam is called "fiqh."

However, times have changed since the life of Muhammad. Inevitably, situations arise that the Qur'an and the hadith do not address. For example, is in vitro fertilization permissible for a married couple to have a child? When confronting a new situation, Muslim legal scholars first review what the Qur'an and hadith have to say on the subject. If they cannot find enough information there, they reason by analogy from the sources and consider the consensus of the Muslim community on the issue. If necessary, they will use their own independent reasoning to make decisions about the correct course of action. The practice of reasoning independently from Islamic principles in order to deal with new issues is called "ijtehad." It does not always lead to agreement. In the case of in vitro fertilization, some scholars may consider it forbidden, while many others may judge it to be permissible, depending on the circumstances.

Shari'a is not intended to be a rigid system. Exceptions to seemingly inflexible rules can be made because of specific individual circumstances or the good of the community.[1] For example, there would be no punishment for those who eat prohibited foods by mistake, because they are starving, or because they are forced to do so by someone else.

Right and Wrong and in Between

In general, the "right path" is anything which is not specifically forbidden by the Qur'an or the Sunnah. Activities not forbidden are called "halal." Examples of halal actions are giving money to charity above and beyond zakat, practicing the five pillars of the faith, doing honest work, participating in marriage and family life, and dressing modestly.

Prohibited activities are called "haram." Examples of haram actions include using alcohol or any other intoxicant, accepting interest on money, eating forbidden foods, having sex outside of marriage, and gambling. Being cruel to animals, being unkind to other people, behaving unethically in business, and gossiping are also haram.

Other behaviors may be recommended ("manduh"), tolerated ("mubah"), or not recommended ("makruh"). Music spans all of these categories. Muhammad felt that listening to women singing solos or flute and stringed instruments caused listeners to turn to sensual thoughts that could result in improper actions. This kind of music is "makruh." However, certain kinds of music, such as group singing and percussion instruments used in narrative songs and celebratory music were "manduh," or encouraged. Popular music is usually considered "mubah." The lines between the different categories of music are not always clear both in the past and in the present. The increase in popular music around the world can cause dissent between Muslim teenagers and their parents. Such disagreements occur in non-Muslim families as well!

> When confronting a new situation, Muslim legal scholars first review what the Qur'an and hadith have to say on the subject.

Punishment

Punishment is meted out under Islamic law for three reasons:

1. It creates a fear of punishment that protects society from crime by deterring criminals. To make sure that everyone knows what the punishment is for a crime, the Qur'an requires that all punishments be carried out in public.

2. Punishments (except the death penalty) are designed to reform the criminal. This is based on the concern that the Qur'an has for creating a just and safe society, as well as the importance it assigns to doing what God wants. The Qur'an

states repeatedly that God will forgive anyone who is truly sorry for doing something bad, no matter how terrible the deed is.

3. There are natural and proper results of all our actions, good and bad. A bad deed results in a bad result, punishment. Criminals should not be able to escape the consequences of their acts.[2]

Crimes that threaten the stability of society are considered extremely serious. These are the crimes that undermine marriage, threaten the family, inhibit possession of property, or incite violence. Punishments for these serious crimes are called "hudud," and are set forth in the Qur'an: one hundred lashes for adultery or improper sexual activity, eighty lashes for making false accusations that someone is unchaste, and amputation of a hand or hands for theft. Murder can be punished by death in extreme circumstances.

Some of the punishments may seem harsh. In Muhammad's time, they were actually considered too lenient. Later Muslim rulers instituted more severe penalties. Today, it has been pointed out that in Saudi Arabia, where amputation of a hand is the standard punishment for theft, store owners can safely leave their businesses open and unattended when they go to the mosque at prayer time.[3] The deterrent effect of the punishment appears to be working. A similar argument about the power of deterrence is used in the United States to support the death penalty.[4]

But the Qur'an also prescribes mercy. If a person kills another in self-defense, or if the dead person's relatives forgive the killer, the punishment will be lighter. So even the stringent Qur'anic punishments allow for some leeway.[5]

"Tazir" is the name given to punishments for lesser crimes. The specific tazir for an action is decided by a judge, and may include jail time and monetary fines. There is a great deal of flexibility in these punishments. Their severity depends on the intent of the criminal in committing the action, the need to have a safe society, and the rights of the individual.[6]

Origins of Islamic Law

Islam originated in an environment of tribal custom. The survival and honor of the family and the tribe or clan were of utmost importance. Revenge was the accepted way to defend the clan and family. Raiding other clans was an accepted way to

A family in Saudi Arabia gathers for a meal. The origins of Islamic law lie in the traditions of the clan, or extended family, which is valued over the individual.

keep your own group alive. Some of the laws in the Qur'an specifically address these tribal ways of life and try to change them for the better. For example, the Qur'an says that the ummah, the community of all Muslims, is the basic unit of society, not the tribe. Thus it tried to place limits on the scope of revenge killings, which otherwise created a constant cycle of murder between clans.

However, the Qur'an does not get rid of all aspects of tribal custom. It allows the heirs of a murdered person to put the killers to death, but sets limits on how this punishment may be imposed. It recommends that murderers be brought to justice by government authorities, not families. The Qur'an also says that monetary payments instead of execution may be made in certain circumstances to the families of murder victims. Such payments were usually allowed when the killing was accidental. In actual practice today, revenge killings are outlawed by national laws in every country.

The Qur'an's stand on punishment for murder echoes the law of retribution that the Torah, the Jewish scripture, preached. Both scriptures place strict limits on the extent of punishment, to keep it from going on from generation to generation. The Qur'an also says, "But whoso forgoes it [retaliation], it shall be an expiation for him." (5:45) Thus, in theory, Muslims are allowed, according to the Qur'an, to seek revenge for the murder of family members, as long as they go through proper channels. A better way, however, is to renounce revenge. This brings expiation, the forgiveness by God of other misdoings for the person who gives up revenge, according to the Qur'an. Muslims are encouraged to renounce bloodshed and to trust God to provide justice.

Who Decides?

The Islamic legal system may seem rather informal compared to the many-layered system in the United States. Scholars, not lawyers, make the decisions in Islamic legal disputes. Sometimes the judges are formally appointed by a government; in other instances, they are acclaimed as authorities by a majority of Muslims in the town, city, or country. They have studied the Qur'an, the hadith, and the vast Islamic legal tradition in recognized Islamic universities for at least five years. Most Muslim scholars working in the United States have been trained in other countries. A few Islamic colleges have been founded in the United States in recent decades. They are beginning the task of providing the detailed training necessary to interpret the complex system of Islamic laws in an American environment.

Muslims are not allowed to take the law into their own hands. Wars may only be declared by a legitimate government. Also, only a religious scholar can issue a fatwa, a legal ruling, based on the principles of Islamic law. Osama bin Laden has issued fatwas calling Muslims to violence against the United States and Israel. Bin Laden is a political figure, not a religious leader, though he uses religious language to promote his cause. Since he is not a recognized Islamic scholar, his pronouncements are not binding on Muslims. Even the Taliban refused to follow his fatwas.[7]

Shari'a Among Sunni and Shi'a Muslims

In Sunni Islam, a group of religious scholars called the "Ulama" is responsible for interpreting the guidelines. These scholars do not make new doctrines, for the Qur'an and the Sunnah are considered to contain everything needed by a Muslim. The scholars of the Ulama are trained in Muslim colleges and work independently. There is no center from which religious doctrine is issued. This is different from the Catholic Church, for example, which looks to the Vatican in Rome for guidance. Given the fact that the Ulama scholars are independent, it is not surprising that differences of opinion have arisen over the years.

Sunni Muslims have developed four schools of legal interpretation. The differences among these schools are very slight.

Shi'as also do not seek to create new doctrines but try to interpret the Qur'an and Sunnah using the same methods that the Sunnis do. Shi'a Islam makes use of additional traditions from the Imams and Ali, the fourth caliph, and his descendants.

Islamic Law in Muslim Countries

Different Muslim countries practice varied interpretations of shari'a. Some have chosen to integrate Islamic religious principles into their legal systems. Others exclude them completely. Not infrequently, religious laws take precedence over the civil legal system.

Pakistan, a Sunni Muslim country, actually has two legal systems, one secular and one religious. The two systems are intertwined, but sometimes they come to different and confusing conclusions. Mirza Tahir Hussain, a British citizen living in Pakistan, was sentenced to death by the non-religious court system in 1989 for killing a taxi driver. After appeals and retrials, he was acquitted on all charges in 1996. However, his case was then turned over to the shari'a court system because his crime was suddenly deemed to be a religious offense, armed robbery. This court sentenced Tahir to death again. Then, in November 2006, Pervez Musharraf, the secular president of Pakistan, commuted his sentence, and Hussain was released.[8]

In Afghanistan, another Sunni country, six men were arrested by Afghan police in April 2005 for stoning to death a woman they believed had committed adultery. One of the men arrested was the woman's father. A religious judge is said to have condemned her to death. The woman's mother did not grieve over her daughter but said, "My daughter was a criminal and a sinner who brought dishonor on my name." The men are awaiting trial. Adultery stirs up strong feelings in Pakistan as well: A couple was shot to death when they were found together in a field. They were both married to other people. Three villagers killed them.[9]

The government of Iran, a Shi'ite country, has proposed a new law to encourage Iranians to wear clothing they deem Islamic. The law will not say precisely what kinds of clothes are suitable, and it will not call for enforcement by police. Its goal is to protect the "Muslim identity" of Iran. However, in the past, Iranian women have been harassed by religious police for what they considered to be inappropriate clothing.[10] And in May 2006, three men were pulled out of their car and shot to death in Baghdad, Iraq. Their crime? Wearing shorts. They were tennis players on their way to a match. The Iraqi government said it was not behind the shootings.[11]

A Special Case; Wahhabism in Saudi Arabia

The Arabian Sheikh Muhammad ibn Abd al-Wahhab (c. 1700–1792) tried to reform Sunni Islam during his long life. He rejected any innovations that had taken place in Islam after about 950 C.E. and preached what he thought was the original, strict form of Islam. He refused to allow his followers to interpret or adapt Islamic teachings as times changed. He said other Muslims who did not follow his lead were worse than non-Muslims. He called on his followers to wage a holy war against them as well as all non-Muslims. He instituted a very strict form of Islamic law.

Followers of Abd al-Wahhab are called Wahhabis. The kingdom of Saudi Arabia is the only country that officially follows this interpretation of Islam. No other religions are allowed. In Saudi Arabia two police forces exist, one governmental and the other religious. Both exercise power at will. Shi'ites are not considered the legal equals of Sunnis. Women cannot vote and must be veiled whenever they appear in public. Men and women may not be together in public places, including schools. A horrifying consequence of this law occurred in March 2002, when a fire broke out in a school in Mecca. The doors were locked in order to keep girls and boys separated. Fifteen girls died.[12]

King Abdullah of Saudi Arabia has attempted to change the implementation of law in his country since he became king in 2005. He has recommended that girls and boys be educated together. Women are being encouraged to apply for drivers' licenses, although they cannot actually drive yet. However, the government's written laws are not often enforced because of the power of the religious establishment.[13]

Islamic Law in Non-Muslim Countries

Muslims constitute significant minorities in many other countries, eastern as well as western. Tensions over interpretation and adherence to Islamic law can arise in these countries. Muslims generally follow the laws of the countries in which they live, unless the laws interfere with the practice of their religion.

A thirteen-year-old British girl, Shabina Begum, asked to be allowed to wear a headscarf and a loose dress that concealed her body to her school. The school refused, so she went to court. After several appeals, the highest court in England ruled in the school's favor. Shabina now attends another school that allows her to dress the way she wants.[14]

In France, external signs of religious affiliation were banned in schools in 2004. Crucifixes, skullcaps, and headscarves were all prohibited. The Muslim community felt that it was the target of the ban, and launched large demonstrations. The government did not back down.[15]

Aspects of Islamic Law

Money in Islam. Islam strictly forbids receiving interest on money that one lends. The Qur'an states: "Allah has allowed trading and forbidden usury." (2:275) This law was pronounced because of the burden that paying interest places on people, especially poor people.

Observance of this fourteen hundred-year-old law causes difficulties for Muslims today. For many years, Muslims who wanted to buy homes saved their money and paid cash. Rising house prices in the twenty-first century make this process too long. But banks have created a solution. It is called "murabaha," or installment financing. A bank in Chicago called Devon serves as an example of how murabaha works. When a customer finds a home, Devon buys the house that the customer wants. It then sells shares of the property to the customer at a price that includes a fee; over time, ownership is transferred to the customer. The total cost to the customer is similar to what would be owed to a bank with interest, but because of the co-ownership arrangement, the customer does not deal with interest.[16]

Islamic banking is big business. It started in 1994 in Malaysia. In 2005, 265 Islamic banks were operating in forty countries, controlling $262 billion dollars. Many Western banks such as Citicorp now have Islamic banking departments. Muslims appreciate the fact that Islamic financial institutions also pay zakat, charitable donations, on their holdings.[17]

Female Circumcision. Some people wonder whether so-called female circumcision, also called female genital cutting or genital mutilation, is common in Muslim societies. The act involves removing some of a woman's external sexual organs. Some cultures believe that such mutilation is necessary to make women chaste before marriage and faithful afterward. This custom is found mostly in some parts of Africa, the Middle East, and South Asia, although it has been practiced in other areas. It existed long before Islam came into being and is not part of the Muslim faith. Some Coptic Christians and tribal Africans are known to practice it. It is practiced to an unknown extent in Western communities consisting of immigrants from countries where it is common.[18] Islamic scholars have largely condemned it, stating that Muhammad himself discouraged it.

However, some Muslims have come to believe that female genital mutilation is a harmless traditional practice. In Egypt, doctors perform most of these procedures. In 2006 it was estimated that over 2 million girls suffered genital mutilation in countries around the world.[19]

Islamic Bioethics. As medical science has advanced, questions about allowing the terminally ill to die without lifesaving measures, how to determine brain death, organ donation, artificial conception, and abortion have all become more and more difficult to answer for everyone. Muslim responses to these issues are based on the Qur'an and Islamic legal tradition.

Suicide is forbidden by the Qur'an, and euthanasia, or assisted death for someone who wishes to die because of a terminal illness, is also forbidden. The Qur'an teaches that the body will be resurrected on the Day of Judgment. Thus cremation is not practiced. Because of this teaching, Muslims did not allow organ donation for a long time. However, recent decisions by international conferences of Muslim legal scholars have allowed organs to be donated when a person is declared brain dead.

Most Islamic scholars believe that the soul does not enter a fetus until about 120 days after conception. Nevertheless, abortion is not allowed even before that date except in some circumstances. According to some, abortion may be permitted in cases of rape. If the mother's life would be endangered by carrying a baby to full term, then abortion is permitted. Couples may practice birth control as long as both husband and wife are in agreement.[20]

"Jihad" means "striving." Commonly, it refers to striving, or struggling if necessary, to do your best in a given arena of life: to be a good student, a good parent, to be generous and unselfish. For Muslims, the way to do this is to follow the Qur'an and the Sunnah, the example set by Muhammad.

Jihad can also describe a struggle or fight against an enemy who attacks you, your family, or your community. The Qur'an says repeatedly that fighting against such opponents is allowed, and also permits battle against someone restricting your freedom: "permission (to fight) is given to those on whom war is made, because they are oppressed." (22:39) The word jihad is not specific to physical combat, but applies to any struggle, whether moral or physical or both. That is why this word was used in the Qur'an, rather than other Arabic words that mean fighting with weapons, such as "harb," "sira'a," "ma'araka," or "qital." It is not one of the five pillars of Islam, but it is an important concept to Muslims.[1]

After Muhammad, the word jihad was misused by some Muslim rulers who fought simply to satisfy their desire for personal power and wealth. They called their military expeditions jihads in order to make their people feel they were justified.[2]

In recent years, the West has heard the word jihad used to mean a Muslim "holy war" waged against perceived adversaries of Muslims all over the world. The violence these jihads involve has often included not just fighting military enemies but terrorism, the killing of innocent civilians. Most Americans

> "Jihad" commonly refers to striving to do your best in a given arena of life; it can also describe a struggle or fight against an enemy.

are confused about the meaning of jihad, and some wonder whether Muslims seek to carry it out in the form of violence.

History records the existence of some violent Muslim groups. For instance, our word "assassin" comes from the Arabic words meaning "hashish eaters." This group of Persian Shi'ites used drugs, despite the Qur'anic injunction against them, to convince themselves to act as suicide killers during the time of the Crusades. In the eleventh and twelfth centuries, the Assassins terrorized the Middle East. They were rejected by mainstream Muslims, and the last leader of the Assassins was executed in 1256. The descendants of these frightening killers now live peacefully in India and some other Middle Eastern countries. Their spiritual leader is the Agha Khan.[3]

At various points in history and in various cultures, suicide killing has been used as a tactic to attack and frighten the enemy. For example, in World War II, some Japanese fighters flew their airplanes into American ships in order to destroy them. These fighters were called kamikazes.

The Greater and Lesser Jihads

Muhammad made a distinction between what he called the "greater jihad" and the "lesser jihad." According to a hadith, one day his followers were returning from a battle, full of the excitement of victory. Muhammad warned them that they were actually leaving the lesser conflict and stepping into the greater, the more important and more difficult battle against negative tendencies in themselves. This battle, not an external conflict but an inner struggle, is the true struggle to which all Muslims are called.[4]

What Does the Qur'an Say About War?

The Qur'an distinguishes clearly between murder and killing an enemy in war. It prescribes punishment for those who intentionally murder others outside of the battlefield: "Whoever kills a person, except as a punishment for murder or villainy in the land, shall be looked upon as though he had killed all mankind." (5:32)

The Qur'an's commands concerning murder never changed. However, its views on battle and war evolved over the twenty-three years that Muhammad recorded it. Because Islam was born in the warlike, lawless society of Arabia, fighting was inevitable. No rules existed to protect civilians or prisoners of war. Tribal practices of vendetta and raiding were the norm. Furthermore, the area was caught between the power-seeking rulers of two empires, Byzantium and Persia. It is not surprising that the Qur'an has a lot to say about war.

When Muhammad and his followers moved to Medina in 622, the small group of Muslims had to fight against those who had driven them out of Mecca in order to survive. It was at this point that Muhammad received verse 22:39 of the Qur'an, which clearly allowed Muslims to conduct defensive, or "just," wars: "Permission (to fight) is given to those on whom war is made, because they are oppressed."[5]

The Qur'an tells Muslims that they must take active measures to protect themselves, and not wait for God to act: "Surely Allah changes not the condition of a people, until they change their own condition." (3:11) An even stronger verse reads: "Fighting is obligatory for you, much as you dislike it." (2:216) Thus the Qur'an does not forbid war as a way to protect people and groups.

It does not, however, allow the lawless, bloody clan battles to continue. Muslims were not to be the aggressors: "Fight for the sake of God those that fight against you, but do not attack them first. God does not love aggressors." (2:190) The Qur'an also restricts violence after a battle has been won and prescribes humane treatment for prisoners of war. Muslims were not allowed to pursue the common practice of enslaving people captured in war, and Muhammad did not allow his followers to kill prisoners of war.

Muslims were not to fight against the Jews and the Christians, who are close religious cousins: "And argue not with the People of the Book ... save such of them as act unjustly." (29:46) The creation of the state of Israel in 1948 resulted in an officially Jewish state covering much of Palestine, including Jerusalem, a city held sacred by Muslims. Many Muslims consider the existence of Israel to be a painful and insulting loss of territory and prestige. They blame both Israel and its supporters for displacing the Palestinians, who are mostly Muslim or Christian, and reducing them to poverty. What was originally a political and economic battle over the status of the Palestinians has been given a strong religious slant.[6]

Does the Qur'an Require "Holy War"?

Does the Qur'an demand that Muslims go to war in support of their religion? If Muslims cannot practice Islam in the way they would like, are they justified in using violence to achieve their goal? Can Muslims fight to force others to convert to Islam?

The statements in the Qur'an on this topic appear confusing and even contradictory. Compare 47:4: "When you meet the unbelievers in the battlefield, strike off their heads and when you have laid them low, bind your captives firmly" with 8:61: "And if they incline to peace, incline thou also to it, and trust in Allah."

These verses must be understood in terms of the experiences of Muhammad and the early community. Since that time, Islamic law and Muslim tradition have developed guidelines and regulations that address the question of jihad. For example, Muslim scholars state that Muslims today must abide by the law of the land in which they reside, and changes must be instituted in society through proper legal and social mechanisms. Muslims must cooperate with others and contribute to the societies in which they live. As long as Muslims are free to practice their faith, they may not cause unrest. Furthermore, while Muslims do wish to share the teachings of their faith with others, they do not believe in forcing others to convert to Islam.

Today, Muslims have many sharply different views on the issue of whether violence and terrorism, including suicide bombing, are appropriate ways to promote and defend Islam. Some feel that terrorist actions are justified when Muslims are being oppressed, whether through violence or through lack of acceptance. Others feel that violence can only be used when Muslims are under actual physical attack. Still others say that suicide bombings are never justified, pointing to the Islamic prohibition against suicide and the killing of innocent people. As an example of the disagreement on this issue, while a handful of Muslims praised the September 11, 2001, attacks on the World Trade Center and the Pentagon in the United States, most prominent Islamic scholars and leaders around the world denounced the suicide bombers.[7]

Al-Qaeda

Those who use the term jihad to justify violence and terrorism do not always share the same goals. Some want to impose militant versions of Islam on their own countries and punish Muslim countries that do not follow their ideas of Islam. Probably the best-known of these groups claiming justification for violence in the Qur'an is al-Qaeda. The name means "the base." This group was created by a wealthy Saudi, Osama bin Laden, in 1988. Its goal is to create fundamentalist Muslim states that follow the Wahhabi ideals. Al-Qaeda wishes to remove all Western military presence and cultural influence from these states. The United States is seen as the most harmful of Western states, so it receives the most attention. Al-Qaeda believes the state of Israel should not exist. It is also willing to punish and even kill Muslims who do not share its views. Al-Qaeda does not hesitate to use terror tactics to gain attention.

Various people have declared jihads against their enemies. However, as with fatwas, only the acknowledged leader of the ummah, the whole Muslim world, can legitimately make such a declaration. There is currently no one leader of the ummah, and no Islamic governments have issued calls to war. Therefore, the jihads we hear about are actually personal vendettas, not "holy wars."[8]

Osama Bin Laden. Osama bin Laden was born in 1957 in Saudi Arabia. He is one of more than fifty children of Mohammed Awad bin Laden. His father ran a construction business worth many millions of dollars, which his children inherited when he died in a helicopter crash in 1968.

The younger bin Laden was educated as an engineer. While at college, he was influenced by a Muslim teacher who wanted to strengthen Wahhabism in Saudi Arabia and to make the country free of all Western influences. When the Soviet Union invaded Afghanistan in 1979, bin Laden went to neighboring

Pakistan to help the Afghan resistance. The CIA trained him and his followers to oppose the Soviets. Bin Laden contributed large amounts of his personal fortune to the Afghan fighters.

When the conflict ended in 1989, bin Laden returned to Saudi Arabia. There he criticized the ruling family of Saudi Arabia for their close ties to the West, particularly the United States. Bin Laden and his family moved to Sudan in 1991 because of threats from the Saudi government.

He had begun establishing the al-Qaeda network when he was in Afghanistan. In Sudan he expanded this network and focused on attacking what he saw as the enemy of Islam, the United States. Al-Qaeda's first terrorist attack came in 1992. In 1993, six people were killed when a bomb exploded in the basement parking garage of the World Trade Center in New York City. The United States grew increasingly concerned about al-Qaeda and anti-U.S. sentiment in the region when eighteen United States soldiers were killed by guerillas in Mogadishu, Somalia.

The Sudanese government asked bin Laden to leave in 1996. By this time the Saudi Arabian government had frozen his assets and his family had disowned him. He returned to Afghanistan and built a relationship with the Taliban that enabled him to train militants. Currently, he remains in hiding, probably along the Afghan-Pakistan border.[9]

Other Groups That Claim Jihad Is Their Duty

Some groups with Islamic affiliations claim to focus more on making social and political reforms in their countries than on imposing strict Islamic rule or attacking Western ideas, but when they use terrorist tactics such as suicide bombings to promote their agendas they can be very dangerous.

The Muslim Brotherhood of Egypt. This group has been in existence for about eighty years. Initially the Brotherhood tried to institute Islamic law and stop Western influence in Egypt. Currently it is officially banned, but the government does not actively oppose it. It seeks to work through promoting political reform and changes in social welfare. The Muslim Brotherhood boasts more than eighty members in the Egyptian parliament, and has branches in other countries, including the United States.

Al Gama'a al Islamiyya. The largest militant organization in Egypt maintains a strong connection with al-Qaeda. It has recently renounced terrorist activities.

Hezbollah in Lebanon. This Shi'ite group has ties to Iran and Syria, where large populations of Shi'a Muslims live. It formed in 1982 after Israel invaded Lebanon. Hezbollah receives aid from Iran and in turn has taken hostages in order to pressure Western nations in their dealings with Iran. The group holds several seats in the Lebanese government, but remains an armed group.

Hamas and Islamic Jihad are two Palestinian groups that specifically oppose Israel. Hamas began in 1984 as an alternative to the secular Palestine Liberation Organization and won control of the Palestinian government in elections held in 2006. Western countries stopped sending aid to the Palestinian government after these elections because Hamas would not renounce violence and refused to recognize Israel as a legitimate state. Islamic Jihad is backed by Syria and Iran. It frequently sends suicide bombers to attack Israel. A branch of Islamic Jihad exists in Egypt, organized by Osama bin Laden's lieutenant, Ayman al Zawahri. The slow pace of peace talks between Israel and the Palestinians enables these groups to attract support from Palestinians who feel hopeless and abandoned.

Jemaah Islamiah is an Indonesian group trying to remove what it feels are pagan practices in South Asian Muslim worship and to oust Western influence from Indonesia. Three members of this group were convicted of killing 202 people and injuring 209 more in three bombings in 2002 on the Indonesian island of Bali.

Religion and Politics

A recent *Newsweek* survey confirms that over three fourths of Americans describe themselves as spiritual, seeking a personal relationship with the divine. Almost two thirds say they are religious, meaning they hold specific beliefs about God.[10] Karen Armstrong, who wrote an important biography of the prophet Muhammad, suggests that interest in religion has been on the upswing all around the world since the 1960s.[11] It is natural to expect that a growing emphasis on religious values will have an effect on politics.

Muslims have always considered involvement in politics to be a religious duty, because they believe that spiritual beliefs must be accompanied by action. The Qur'an states: "O you who believe, be maintainers of justice." (4:135) This duty finds expression in the strong sense of social responsibility that pervades Islam.

Many Muslims living in countries with non-religious governments are active in promoting legislation on the local and national levels that attempts to curb excessive drinking, pornography, and violence, just to name a few examples. They also support causes such as better access to medical care, excellence in education, and humane treatment of animals. Muslims take positions on these issues from a personal as well as a religious perspective.

Islam is claiming more and more observant followers in Western countries, especially the United States. Younger American Muslims are more likely to attend the mosque weekly and pray five times a day than their parents.[12] They are likely to bring a Muslim perspective into the voting booth, just as the votes of Christians, Jews, and atheists reflect their philosophies. This perspective is important because Muslims in the United States vote in greater numbers than the population as a whole. Sana Haq, an American teenager born in the United States to Pakistani immigrant parents, is a young but typical example. She goes to the mall to buy jeans and loves her new driver's license, like most Americans her age. However, she also describes herself as Muslim first, and everything else second. "Muslim. It's the most important thing to me," she says.[13] When she turns eighteen next year, she will probably vote in accordance with her Muslim ideals.

Muslim countries are also seeing religious revivals that translate into political action. The effects have sometimes been violent. In countries such as Egypt and Algeria, the secular governments have failed to create social stability or economic growth and are usually undemocratic and oppressive. Citizens feel that they have few opportunities and little voice in world affairs. They feel overrun and undervalued by Western countries, especially the United States. In these political climates, a call to "return to Islam" is very appealing. It promises social equality, economic fairness, and complete rejection of foreign, meaning Western, values.[14]

In other Muslim countries, religious revival translates into a return to what many see as a narrow-minded interpretation of Islam. Since American and other forces invaded Iraq in 2003, the strict enforcement of Islamic law by various groups has increased. A young Iraqi woman using the pseudonym "Riverbend" writes that women in Baghdad now may not leave their homes alone. More and more women wear headscarves and clothing that completely covers their bodies, trying to stay safe in an environment where a woman wearing jeans is a target for assault. Because the unemployment rate is 65 percent, many women have lost their jobs. A prominent electrical engineer was killed in Baghdad in early 2006 because she refused to obey conservative extremists who did not want a woman to hold a responsible job. In Afghanistan, although the U.S. is in control of the capital, tribal groups are strong in the countryside. Corruption and a rise in drug smuggling are causing fear and insecurity among inhabitants, and as a result there has been a resurgence in Taliban activity.[15]

Religious revival can also be seen in Egypt, Malaysia, and Turkey. The Muslim Brotherhood won a record eighty-eight seats in the recent parliamentary elections in Egypt.[16] In Malaysia, Hindu protesters demonstrated against what they claimed was the destruction of hundreds of Hindu temples by government authorities. They blamed growing "Islamization" in the country.[17] Even in officially secular Turkey, Islamic parties are electing more and more representatives in parliament.[18]

Dialogue

Because of the growing interest in religion, many people are trying to engage in dialogue on religious issues. Comedian Albert Brooks has released a film entitled *Looking for Comedy in the Muslim World*. The movie depicts an American comedian who was sent to India and Pakistan to try to improve American-Muslim relations by finding out what makes Muslims laugh. Brooks says the movie contains no religious references at all, but the studio he originally contracted with refused to release the picture, and Brooks had to find another, smaller distributor.[19]

Horace Ballard knew what being different was like. He was the only black student in his elementary school in Bath, Pennsylvania, and he was a Muslim as well. He got a lot of strange looks and questions. He chose to respond with information instead of anger. When he got to the University of Virginia shortly after the September 11 attacks, he found students horrified, confused, and angry about what had happened. He organized a poetry reading through the Muslim Student Alliance to raise issues surrounding Islam, violence, and diversity. This one effort by one person has now turned into the Poetry for Peace Project, which uses poetry and drama to ease tensions about racial and ethnic issues.[20]

Since the September 11 attacks, attempts at dialogue among Jewish, Christian, and Muslim groups have increased. Officials from the Vatican, home to the Pope, the leader of the Catholic Church, and from the World Jewish Congress have met and are reaching out to mainstream Muslim leaders.[21] The current leader of the Catholic Church, Pope Benedict XVII, is urging

Two teenage girls—one Jewish and one Muslim—chat as they help out at a New Jersey homeless shelter. Many people believe that dialogue is the key to understanding between different religious groups.

the United States to seek a peaceful solution to the issue of nuclear capability in Iran.

In Africa, Muslims typically live harmoniously with those of other faiths. In Madagascar, Muslims donated land for a Christian church in the town of Ambilobe.[22] In Ethiopia's Danakil desert, Muslims and Christians work together to mine salt left behind by ancient oceans at Lake Asele.[23] And in Nigeria, a Muslim woman was sentenced to death for adultery after reporting that she had been raped. The Catholic archbishop of Lagos, Anthony Olubummi Okogie, spoke at her trial and quoted the Qur'an in her support. She was ultimately released.[24]

The West and Islam ignore each other at their peril. The number of Muslims in the world is growing rapidly, and the size and breadth of the Muslim community demands recognition. The non-Muslim West is no longer the only economic power in the world. Prejudice is frequently built on ignorance. Muslims and non-Muslims benefit from information and education about each other. The fact that a person follows a particular religion does not mean that the person adheres to a given set of customs. Understanding and accepting the cultures of others, and realizing that customs are not always religiously based in Muslim or non-Muslim communities, helps everyone live together much more harmoniously. Reaching out to one another, perhaps stretching beyond our comfort zones, gives us the opportunity to change for the better our lives as individuals and the world as a whole.

Chapter Notes

Chapter 1 What Is Islam?

1. John L. Esposito, *What Everyone Needs to Know About Islam* (New York: Oxford University Press, 2002), pp. 1–2.

2. Charles E. Cobb, Jr., "Africa in Fact," *National Geographic*, September 2005, "Geographica" section, p. 2.

3. "Europe's Muslims," *Economist*, August 10, 2002, pp. 10–11.

4. Jerry Adler, "Special Report: Spirituality 2005," Newsweek, August 29–September 5, 2005, p. 52.

5. "The Largest Muslim Communities," *Adherents.com*, 2005, <http://www.adherents.com/largecom/com_islam.html> (May 8, 2006).

6. "Image: Islam percentage by country.png," *Wikipedia*, n.d., <http://en.wikipedia.org/wiki/Image:Islam_percentage_by_country.png> (August 23, 2007).

7. Esposito, p. 71.

8. "The Reluctant Heroine; A Conversation with a Nobel Peace Prize Winner," *Azizah*, December 2004–January 2005, p. 39.

9. Bill Powell, "Generation Jihad," *Time*, October 3, 2005, p. 59.

10. "Islamic Extremism: Common Concern for Muslim and Western Publics," *The Pew Global Attitudes Project*, July 14, 2005, <http://pewglobal.org/reports/display.php?ReportID=248> (June 9, 2006).

11. Toni Locy, "Patriot Act Blurred in the Public Mind," *USA Today*, February 26, 2004, p. A5.

12. Martin H. Singer, "U.S. Must Welcome Immigrants with Special Skills," *Chicago Sun-Times*, May 14, 2006, <http://www.suntimes.com/output/otherviews/cst-cont-workers14.html> (May 24, 2006).

13. Marc Lynch, "Watching al-Jazeera," *The Wilson Quarterly*, Summer 2005, Vol. 29, No. 3, pp. 36–45; Jeremy Scahill, "The War on Al Jazeera," *The Nation*, December 12, 2005, Vol. 281, No. 21, pp. 6–8.

14. Jim Lobe, "Evangelical Christians Most Distrustful of Muslims," *Global Information Network*, March 23, 2006, p. 1.

15. "Unequal Protection: The Status of Muslim Civil Rights in the United States," *Council on American Islamic Relations*, May 2005, <http://www.cair-net.org/asp/2005CivilRightsReport.pdf> (June 9, 2006).

16. "Frank S. Roque," *azcentral.com*, special report, June 22, 2004, <http://www.azcentral.com/specials/special32/articles/08030622ro que-ON.html> (May 16, 2006).

17. Patricia Smith, "Islam in America," *New York Times*, January 9, 2006, pp. 10–15.

18. Paul Findley, *Silent No More: Confronting America's False Images of Islam* (Beltsville, Md.: Amana Publications, 2001), pp. 71–74.

19. "Islamic Extremism: Common Concern for Muslim and Western Publics."

Chapter 2 Origins and Early History of Islam

1. Karen Armstrong, *Muhammad* (New York: Harper San Francisco, 1992), pp. 101–107.

2. Ibid., p. 50.

3. "Koran Desecration Unleashes Muslim Anger," *UPI* Perspectives, May 2005, <http://www.accessmylibrary.com/coms2/summary_0286-6570813_ITM> (June 28, 2007).

4. Armstrong, p. 101.

5. Akbar S. Ahmed, *Islam Today* (New York: I.B. Tauris, 2002), p. 19.

6. John Esposito, *Islam: The Straight Path* (New York: Oxford University Press, 1991), pp. 37–40.

7. Solomon Moore, "Al-Zarqawi Urges Sunnis to 'Confront Shiite Snakes,'" *The Morning Call*, Page A2, June 3, 2006.

8. Aatif Ali Bokhari, "No Shi'a-Sunni Split Here," *The Arab American News*, March 4–10, 2006, p. 14.

Chapter 3 Beliefs and Practices of Islam

1. "Women's Work," *Economist*, December 1, 2001, p. 45.

2. Yahiya Emerick, *What Islam Is All About* (Livonia, Mich.: Noorart, 2004), pp. 147–150.

3. Ibid., pp. 158–160.

4. "A History of Hajj Tragedies," *The Guardian*, January 13, 2006, <http://www.guardian.co.uk/international/story/0,,1685222,00.html> (June 8, 2006).

5. Caesar E. Farah, *Islam: Beliefs and Observances*, Seventh Edition (New York: Barron's Educational Series, 2003), pp. 115–119.

Chapter 4 Religious and Cultural Customs Among Muslims

1. Luke Harding and Kim Willsher, "Anger as Papers Reprint Cartoons of Muhammad," *The Guardian*, February 2, 2006, <http://www.guardian.co.uk/religion/Story/0,,1700224,00.html> (February 2, 2006).

2. Karen Armstrong, *Muhammad* (New York: Harper San Francisco, 1992), pp. 197–198.

3. *Muhammad, Legacy of a Prophet*, video produced by Alexander Kronemer and Michael Wolfe, Kikim Media, 2002; Shahnaz Taplin Chinoy, "Benign in Bombay, Charged in France; Can We Stereotype a Woman Wearing a Burqua or Hijab?" *India Currents*, February 2006, p. 10.

4. "A Look at the Wearing of Veils, and Disputes on the Issue, Across the Muslim World," *International Herald Tribune*, October 31, 2006, <http://www.iht.com/bin/print.php?id=3344621> (April 21, 2007).

5. Steve Tamari, "Who Are the Arabs?" Center for Contemporary Arab Studies, Georgetown University, n.d., <http://ccas.georgetown.edu/files/who_are_arabs.pdf> (April 20, 2007).

6. "Introduction to Islam," *About: Islam*, n.d., <http://islam.about.com/od/basicbeliefs/p/intro.htm> (May 24, 2006); John L. Esposito, *What Everyone Needs to Know About Islam* (New York: Oxford University Press, 2002), p. 2.

7. Joyce Howard Price, "1.2 Million Arabs in U.S., Census States," *The Washington Times*, December 3, 2003, <http://washington times.com/functions/print/php?Story ID=20031203-113839-9531r> (April 21, 2007).

8. Margaret Nydell, *Understanding Arabs* (Boston: Intercultural Press, 2005), pp. 23–25.

9. Caesar E. Farah, *Islam: Beliefs and Observances*, Seventh Edition (New York: Barron's Educational Series, 2003), pp. 22–25.

10. Richard D. Connerney, "Islam: Religion of the Sword?" *Salon.com*, October 11, 2001, <http://archive.salon.com/news/feature/2001/10/11/sword/index.html> (May 10, 2006).

11. Teresa Watanabe, "Interpreting Islam: War and Peace," *Los Angeles Times*, October 5, 2001.

12. "Rif Berbers," *YWAM Sahara*, n.d., <http://www.gosahara.org/rb.html> (May 17, 2006); "Sudan—Religion," Sudan: A Country Study, Helen Chapin Metz, ed., 1991, <http://countrystudies.us/sudan/47.html> (May 17, 2006).

13. "Incense, Silk and Jihad," *Economist*, May 31, 2003, pp. 37–39.

14. Gregg Zoroya, "Something to Write Home About; Afghans Heap on the Hospitality," *USA Today*, December 21, 2001, p. D.1.

15. Rick Bragg, "Afghan and Pakistani Tribe Lives by its Guns and Honor," *New York Times*, October 21, 2001, p. 1A1.

16. Waldemar Januszczak, "The Price of Peace Between Christianity and Islam?" *The Sunday Times Culture*, May 7, 2006, pp. 10–11.

17. Owen Matthews and Sami Kohen, "Beginning of the End?" *Newsweek*, June 5, 2006, pp. 24–27.

Chapter 5 Women and Islam

1. Muhammad Ali, *The Holy Qur'an with English Translation and Commentary* (Dublin, Ohio: Ahmadiyya Anjuman Isha'at Islam Lahore Inc., USA, 2002), footnote 34e, p. 206.

2. Yahiya Emerick, *What Islam Is All About* (Livonia, Mich.: Noorart, 2004), p. 272.

3. John L. Esposito, *What Everyone Needs to Know About Islam* (New York: Oxford University Press, 2002), p. 143.

4. Ali, footnote 35a, p. 207.

5. Kristine Uhlman, "Overview of Shari'a and Prevalent Customs in Islamic Societies—Divorce and Child Custody," *ExpertLaw*, January 2004, <http://www.expertlaw.com/library/family_law/islamic_custody-3.html> (April 21, 2007).

6. Ali, footnote 227a, p. 101.

7. Mohamed S. El-Awa, "Women Imams!" *Al-Ahram Weekly Online*, 2005, <http://weekly.ahram.org.eg/2005/736/op.html> (April 21, 2007).

8. "A Woman's Place," *Economist*, March 19, 2005, p. 10.

9. Suna Erdem, "Islamist Party Divided by MP's Abuse of Wife," *The Times*, May 17, 2006, Overseas News section, p. 35.

10. Samar Fatany, "The Status of Women in Saudi Arabia," *The Arab News*, October 12, 2004, <http://www.arabnews.com/?page=7&section=0&article=52784&d=12&m=10&y=2004> (June 28, 2007).

11. Afshin Molavi, "Young and Restless," *Smithsonian*, April 2006, pp. 68–79.

12. Mody Al-Khalaf, "Women in Saudi Arabia Too Have a Dream," *The Arab News*, November 26, 2004, <http://www.arabnews.com/?page=9&section=0&article=55066&d=26&m=11&y=2004> (June 28, 2007).

13. "Kuwait: Women Gain Political Rights," *Off Our Backs*, May–June 2005, p. 8.

14. "The Reluctant Heroine; A Conversation with a Nobel Peace Prize Winner," *Azizah*, December 2004–January 2005, p. 39.

15. Katherine Zoepf, "Women Fight for Opportunity and Respect at Afghan Universities," *Chronicle of Higher Education*, January 27, 2006, pp. A48–A49.

16. Volume 7, Book 62, Number 69 of the hadith collected by Imam Bukhari, *University of Southern California Web site*, n.d., <http://www.usc.edu/dept/MSA/fundamentals/hadithsunnah/bukhari/062.sbt.html> (June 28, 2007).

17. Esposito, p. 88.

18. Akbar S. Ahmed, *Islam Today* (New York: I.B. Tauris, 2002), p. 159.

19. Khalid Tanveer, "Honour Killings Stun Pakistan," *Toronto Star*, December 29, 2005, <http://search.ebscohost.com/login.aspx?direct=true&db=nfh&AN=6FP2476458920&site=ehost-live> (April 23, 2007).

20. "Pakistan: Injustice of Honor Killings Continues," *Radio Australia* transcript, May 24, 2006, <http://abc.net.au/ra/asiapac/programs/s1645698.htm> (May 26, 2006).

21. Hillary Mayell, "Thousands of Women Killed for Family 'Honor,'" *National Geographic News*, February 12, 2002, <http://news.nationalgeographic.com/news/2002/02/0212_020212_honorkilling.html> (May 26, 2006).

22. "A Woman's Place."

23. Daniel McGrory, "This Muslim Girl Defied her Father—and her Lover Paid with his Life," *The Times*, November 11, 2005, <www.timesonline.co.uk/tol/news/uk/article586736.ece> (June 28, 2007).

24. "Germany: Muslim Women Killed by Families," *Off Our Backs*, May–June 2005, pp. 8–9.

Chapter 6 Minorities and Islam

1. "Largest Religious Groups in the United States of America," *Adherents.com*, 2005, <http://www.adherents.com/rel_USA.html> (May 8, 2006).

2. Anayat Durrani, "Islam in the U.S.," <http://www.suite101.com/article.cfm.islam_in_the_us/33392/1> (May 8, 2006).

3. Jerry Adler, "Special Report: Spirituality 2005," *Newsweek*, August 29 –September 5, 2005, p. 54; John Dart, "Muslim Numbers Disputed," Christian Century, November 14, 2001, pp. 9–10.

4. Patricia Smith, "Islam in America," *New York Times*, January 9, 2006, pp. 10–15.

5. Sylviane A. Diouf, *Servants of Allah: African Muslims Enslaved in*

the Americas (New York: New York University Press, 1998), pp. 4, 48–49.

6. Cara Anna, "Muslim Sorority Aims to Enhance Greek Scene," *The Charlotte Observer*, November 27, 2005, p. B3.

7. Mary Rourke, "Muslim Students in California," U.S. Department of State's Bureau of International Information Programs, n.d., <http://usinfo.state.gov/products/pubs/muslimlife/castudent.html> (May 29, 2006).

8. Niraj Warikoo, "Students Get Taste of Muslim Customs: Metro Detroiters Reenact Hajj Rituals," *Knight Ridder Tribune Business News*, January 10, 2006, p. 1.

9. Phyllis McIntosh, "Native Deen's Muslim Rap," U.S. Department of State's Bureau of International Information Programs, n.d., <http://usinfo.state.gov/products/pubs/muslimlife/rap.html> (May 29, 2006).

10. "African-American Muslims," *About: Islam*, n.d., <http://islam.about.com/library/weekly/aa012601c.htm> (April 24, 2006).

11. Yahiya Emerick, *What Islam Is All About* (Livonia, Mich.: Noorart, 2004), p. 285.

12. Malcolm X with Alex Haley, *The Autobiography of Malcolm X* (New York: Ballantine Books, 1987).

13. Michele Norris, "Profile: How European Muslims View Themselves in the Midst of a Rising Fear of Islamic Fundamentalism in Europe," *NPR, All Things Considered* transcript, December 13, 2004, <http://proquest.umi.com/pdqweb?did=857583161&sid=3&Fmt=1&clientId=5423&RQT=309&VName=PQD> (April 23, 2007).

Chapter 7 Shari'a: Religious Law

1. John L. Esposito, *What Everyone Needs to Know About Islam* (New York: Oxford University Press, 2002), p. 140.

2. "Crime and Punishment in Islam-#3/3," *The Islamic Network*, <http://www.islam.net/main/display_article_id=915> (May 27, 2006).

3. Akbar S. Ahmed, *Islam Today* (New York: I.B. Tauris, 2002), p. 145.

4. Esposito, p. 150.

5. Ahmed, pp. 145–146.

6. "Crime and Punishment in Islam-#3/3."

7. Keira Stevenson, "Osama bin Laden," 2005, <http://search.epnet. com/login.aspx?direct=true&db=f5h8an=17292473> (June 10, 2006).

8. "British Death Row Inmate Freed from Pakistani Prison," *Voice of America News*, November 17, 2006, <http://www.voanews.com/ english/archive/2006-11/2006-11-17voa14.cfm?CFID=37686300 &CFTOKEN=98012086 > (February 21, 2007).

9. "Afghan Woman Executed for Adultery," *Church and State*, June 2005, p. 21; "Couple Shot Dead for Adultery in a Field," *The Guardian*, May 30, 2006, <http://www.guardian.co.uk/pakistan/ Story/0,,1785590,00.html> (May 29, 2006).

10. "Draft Law Urges Iranians to Wear Islamic Clothing," *The Morning Call*, May 21, 2006, p. A5.

11. Kim Gamel, "Extremists Target Iraqi Athletes' Dress," *The Morning Call*, May 28, 2006, p. A4.

12. "Saudi Police 'Stopped' Fire Rescue," *BBC News*, March 15, 2002, <http://news.bbc.co.uk/2/hi/middle_east/1874471.stm> (June 10, 2006).

13. Ibrahim Mugaiteeb, "Saudi Justice," *The Wall Street Journal*, April 15, 2006, p. A7.

14. Jasper Gerard, "Faith, the Veil, Shopping and Me," *The Sunday Times*, March 26, 2006, p. 5.

15. "Minister Blasts Headscarf Protest," *BBC News*, January 18, 2004, <http://news.bbc.co.uk/ 2/hi/Europe/3406969.stm> (June 5, 2006).

16. Janet Ginsburg and Ira Sager, "Koran-Friendly Lenders," *Business Week*, February 14, 2005, p. 12.

17. Assif Shameen, "Islamic Banks: A Novelty No Longer," *Business Week Online*, August 8, 2005, <http://www.businessweek.com/ magazine/content/05_32/b3946141> (May 22, 2006).

18. "Female Genital Mutilation," *BBC News*, December 23, 1998,

<http://news.bbc.co.uk/2/low/health/medical_notes/241221.stm>
(April 19, 2007).

19. Amira El Ahl, "Theologians Battle Female Circumcision," *Spiegel Online*, December 6, 2006, <http://www.spiegel.de/international/spiegel/0,1518,druck-452790,00.html> (April 19, 2007).

20. Esposito, p. 147.

Chapter 8 Jihad or Dialogue?

1. Karen Armstrong, *Muhammad* (New York: Harper San Francisco, 1992), p. 168.

2. Javeed Akhter, "Does Islam Promote Violence?" *International Strategy and Policy Institute*, August 20, 2002, <www.ispi-usa.org> (September 13, 2007).

3. Caesar E. Farah, *Islam*, Seventh Edition (New York: Barron's Educational Series, 2003), pp. 182–183.

4. John L. Esposito, *What Everyone Needs to Know About Islam* (New York: Oxford University Press, 2002), pp. 117–118.

5. Armstrong, pp. 168–169.

6. Akbar S. Ahmed, *Islam Today* (New York: I.B. Tauris, 2002), pp. 134–136.

7. Esposito, pp. 126–127.

8. Yahiya Emerick, *What Islam Is All About* (Livonia, Mich.: Noorart, 2004), pp. 163–164.

9. Keira Stevenson, "Osama bin Laden," 2005, <http://search.epnet.com/login.aspx?direct=true&db=f5h8an=17292473> (June 10, 2006).

10. Jerry Adler, "Special Report: Spirituality 2005," *Newsweek*, August 29–September 5, 2005, p. 48.

11. Karen Armstrong, *The Spiral Staircase* (New York: Knopf, 2004), p. 202.

12. Adler, p. 63.

13. Patricia Smith, "Islam in America," *New York Times*, January 9, 2006, pp. 10–15.

14. Daniel Pipes, "It's Not the Economy, Stupid," *Washington Post*, July 2,

1995, <http://www.danielpipes.org/article/269> (June 2, 2006); George R. Trumbull IV, "Islamic Fundamentalism," *Princeton Journal of Foreign Affairs*, Winter 1998, <http://www.princeton. edu/~foreigna/winter1998/islam.html> (June 2, 2006)

15. "Love and Hate in Baghdad," *The Sunday Times*, April 2, 2006, News Review section, pp. 1–2; Jason Straziuso, "Brazen Taliban Attacks Raise Afghan Fears," May 19, 2006, <http://www.apnews. myway.com//article/200650519/D8HMS1QO0.html> (May 19, 2006).

16. "Broken Promises," *Economist*, April 22, 2006, pp. 48–49.

17. "'Islamization' Blamed for Demolition of Temples," *The Morning Call*, June 3, 2006, p. D11.

18. William Horsley, "Turkish Pro-Islamic Party on the Rise," *BBC News World Edition*, November 4, 2002, <http://news.bbc.co.uk/ 2/hi/europe/2223787.stm> (May 30, 2006).

19. Arthur Spiegelman, "Film with Word 'Muslim' in Title Stirs Controversy," Reuters, September 28, 2005, <http://news.yahoo. com/s/nm/20050928> (September 29, 2005).

20. David Perlmutt, "After 9-11, He Used Poetry Project to Reach Out to Muslims," *Knight Ridder Tribune Business News*, Washington: February 27, 2006, p. 1.

21. Jennifer Siegel, "Jewish, Catholic Leaders Plan Muslim Dialogue," *Forward*, February 24, 2006, p. 9.

22. "Muslims Donate Land for Anglican Church," *Episcopal Life*, April 2006, p. 5.

23. Virginia Morell, "Africa's Danakil Desert, Cruelest Place on Earth," *National Geographic*, October 2005, p. 48.

24. Toye Olori, "Rights-Nigeria: Death Sentence Revoked Against Unwed Mom," *Global Information Network*, March 25, 2002, p.1.

Glossary

burka—A heavy garment that covers a woman's face and body.

deen—Arabic for "way of life," referring to Islam as a comprehensive way to live.

fiqh—Legal interpretations in Islamic law.

Five Pillars of Islam—Basic practices required of all Muslims.

hadith—A story about or saying by Muhammad considered reliable by Islamic scholars.

hajj—One of the five required duties of all Muslims, a pilgrimage to Mecca.

halal—Actions and food permitted by Islamic law.

haram—Actions and food not permitted by Islamic law.

hijab—A scarf that covers a woman's hair, ears, and neck.

Id al Fitr—The feast of fast breaking at the end of Ramadan.

iftar—A small meal eaten after the sun goes down during Ramadan.

ijtehad—The principle of reasoning independently from Islamic precepts.

Islam—The name of a major world religion. It means "submission to God."

jahiliyah—The time before the message of the Qur'an was revealed.

jihad—Literally means "struggle." The word denotes any effort to do right. Some apply it to wars against people they perceive as threatening to Islamic beliefs.

jinn—Supernatural beings created by God from fire. They can obey God or not.

Ka'aba—The sacred building in Mecca, said by Muslims to have been built by the prophet Abraham. Muslim pilgrims walk around it during the hajj.

makruh—Actions that are neither forbidden nor recommended.

masjid—Another name for mosque.

mosque—Center for Muslim prayers.

murabaha—Installment payments that avoid the prohibition against paying interest.

Muslim—One who submits to God.

mutaween—Religious police in Saudi Arabia.

People of the Book—What Muslims call themselves, Jews, and Christians, because they share a common religious heritage.

Qur'an—Revelations received by Muhammad and written down by his companions, believed by Muslims to be the literal word of God.

Ramadan—A month in the Islamic calendar during which Muslims fast during daylight hours.

sahoor—A light breakfast eaten before sunrise during Ramadan.

Salat/Salah—Muslim prayers.

sawm—Fasting during the month of Ramadan

Shahada—The statement of belief made by Muslims.

Shari'a—The "right path," usually used to refer to the Islamic system of laws.

Shi'a—A group of Muslims who believe Muhammad's son-in-law, Ali, was his rightful heir. Shi'ites make up about 15 percent of all Muslims.

Sufi—Muslim mystics.

Sunnah—Muhammad's way of life as recorded in historical accounts and hadith texts. It is meant to be imitated by Muslims.

Sunni—A group of Muslims who believe that the early leaders of Islam were properly chosen and that Muhammad's descendants do not have the exclusive right to head the community. Sunnis constitute about 85 percent of Muslims worldwide.

Taliban—Group of young men that took over the government of Afghanistan from 1996 to 2001 and instituted strict Islamic law.

ummah—The world community of Muslims.

umrah—Visit to Mecca, Medina, or Jerusalem that is separate from the hajj.

Wahhabism—A strict form of Islam practiced in Saudi Arabia.

zakat—Islamic charity, mandated by the Qur'an.

Further Reading

Books

Alkouatli, Claire. *Islam.* Tarrytown, N.Y.: Marshall Cavendish, 2006.

Ernst, Carl W. *Following Muhammed: Rethinking Islam in the Contemporary World.* Chapel Hill, N.C.: University of North Carolina, 2003.

Feener, R. Michael. *Islam in World Cultures: Comparative Perspectives.* Santa Barbara, Calif.: ABC-CLIO, 2004.

Miller, John, and Aaron Kenedi, editors. *Inside Islam: The Faith, the People, and the Conflicts of the World's Fastest-Growing Religion.* New York: Marlowe & Co., 2002.

Siddiqui, Haroon. *Being Muslim.* Toronto: Groundwood Books, 2006.

Whitehead, Kim. *Islam: The Basics.* Broomall, Pa.: Mason Crest Publishers, 2004.

Internet Addresses

CBBC Newsround: Islam
<http://news.bbc.co.uk/cbbcnews/hi/specials/2005/islam/default.stm>

Islam: Empire of Faith
<http://www.pbs.org/empires/islam/>

Muslim Heritage
<http://www.muslimheritage.com/>

Index